LIVE, LOVE, AND LEARN

LIVE, LOVE, AND LEARN

Messages for Women

DESERET
BOOK

SALT LAKE CITY, UTAH

Library of Congress Cataloging-in-Publication Data

Live, love, and learn : messages for women.
   p. cm.
ISBN 978-1-59038-856-3 (hardcover : alk. paper)
1. Mormon women—Religious life. I. Deseret Book Company.
BX8641.L575 2008
242'.643—dc22   2007045764

Printed in the United States of America
R. R. Donnelley and Sons, Crawfordsville, IN

10   9   8   7   6   5   4   3   2   1

CONTENTS

GOD IS HELPING YOU

Mary Ellen Edmunds

One of the most oft-quoted scriptures is 1 Nephi 3:7. Lehi has been commanded by the Lord to send his sons back to Jerusalem to obtain their family records and the writings of the prophets—the brass plates—from Laban. The older brothers have murmured (apparently Lehi shared the news with them first), saying it's a hard thing their father has required of them. Nephi explains that their father is not the one who's requiring it—that it's a command from the Lord. Nephi is willing, and this pleases Lehi, who says that he knows Nephi will be blessed because he hasn't murmured. And then comes Nephi's well-known response in verse 7: "And it came to pass that I, Nephi, said unto my father: I will go and do the things which the Lord hath commanded, for I know that the Lord giveth no commandments unto the children of men, save he shall prepare a way for them that they may accomplish the thing which he commandeth them."

The next verse tells us that Lehi is "exceedingly glad" because he knows that his son Nephi has been blessed of the

Lord. Nephi's response in verse 7 has always impressed me. I want to be this faithful. I want Heavenly Father to be able to depend on me and to ask me to do something and then be confident that I'll do it, even if the command isn't an easy one. I've thought a lot about the blessing that came because Nephi didn't murmur. I'm too often a murmurer (that's a funny word to try to say). I'm working at NOT being a murmurer, and I think I'm making progress.

I want to look at another aspect of the verse. Nephi says that God prepares a way for us to accomplish what He commands us to do. This doesn't mean He performs the tasks for us. Occasionally, I've heard verse 7 interpreted almost that way—as if God gives us things to do and then does them for us. But Nephi said God would prepare a way for *us* to accomplish His will. It has been my experience that our Heavenly Father lets us learn by doing. He allows us to have opportunities to exercise our agency, to choose (often between and among things which are good), increasingly being able to choose the most important things. And he never ever asks us to do something we cannot do, with His help.

Turn to 1 Nephi 17:2 to see what we can learn. Lehi and his family have been out in the wilderness for quite a while by this time. Nephi records that they have waded through much affliction and even that babies had been born. But then he records in verse 2 that "so great were the blessings of the Lord upon us, that while we did live upon raw meat in the wilderness, our women did give plenty of suck for their children, and were strong, yea, even like unto the men; and they began to bear their journeyings without murmurings." These are such wonderful blessings during the eight years they spend in the wilderness. And now comes verse 3 with a great testimony and lesson for us: "And thus we see that the commandments of God must be fulfilled. And if it so be that the children of men keep the commandments of God he doth nourish them, and strengthen them, and provide means whereby they can accomplish the thing which he has commanded them; wherefore, he did provide means for us while we did sojourn in the wilderness."

Eureka! Nephi was right. And he teaches us the way to receive help. We keep the commandments. We refrain from murmuring when He commands us to do something. And then He nourishes us, and blesses us, and provides all that we need in order to accomplish what He has asked. May you feel Him helping with all that is asked of you in this season of your life.

DECIDE ONCE

Don H. Staheli

I have developed a practical approach to hair dryer preservation. In a household with four daughters and a wife, each of whom has thick hair, such imaginative strategies for living are important. Especially if some economic benefit can be realized in the process.

For years we went through hair dryers almost as fast as the cans of spray. I tried to fix them when they broke, but the little busted pieces, essential to the operation of the appliance, were expensive to replace and impossible to rebuild (I think they are built by robots anyway. Nobody has fingers small enough and eyesight so clear as to actually put together the innards of one of these hot-air machines). So, it was off to the discount store to find another 1500 watt beauty.

Finally, one day, I figured it out. There was a common symptom in the early demise of the hair dryers. The heating element rarely seemed to run out of heat. The blower itself looked okay. But the on/off switch—yes the vulnerable switch—was the scene of manipulated mayhem. "On" when the drying started. "Off" to wind a curl or comb a snarl. "On" for more drying and shaping—slow speed for styling, high speed for quicker drying, slow again, then off: a thumb-generated endurance test to which the machine just wasn't equal. No matter the cost of the unit, the switch was often the first thing to go.

The solution was simple. Just turn it on and leave it on. Only move the switch once! Plug it in for power when you want it to blow and unplug it when you're through. Admittedly, this was somewhat impractical for certain hair-dos, but for many needs it was perfect—and with far less thumbing of the on/off button, it lasted much longer.

A lot of our decisions in life can be like that. There is no need to go back and forth or up and down about many things. You just make the decision once and let it go at that. For instance, I feel sorry for those who agonize each Sunday morning over whether or not to go to church that day. Or for those who struggle to obey the Word of Wisdom. Imagine having this argument with yourself, over and over: "Should I drink a beer or should I not? Maybe this time, but not again. Well, perhaps I will. After all, this is a special occasion. No, I really shouldn't drink at all. I guess . . ."

No! Just make up your mind that you are going to do what's best and stick with it. Your decision switch will last a lot longer that way. Of course, there are times when we choose to deviate from our usual way of behaving because the circumstances require a different approach (not with drinking!). But most of the time we need to make up our minds only once, and that decision can then be applied over and over again, generally leading us to do what is right and saving ourselves needless anxiety and turmoil.

Perhaps that is what the Lord meant us to understand when he gave us this principle: "But in case no additional light is given, the first decision shall stand" (D&C 102:22).

ALLOWING TIME FOR CHANGE

Virginia Hinckley Pearce

stepped out into the backyard last night just as evening began to settle. I was just doing some taking and getting, turning off and closing down, when quite suddenly I inhaled. The scent of lilacs filled my whole body and hung almost visibly in the air. Everything seemed to gather around me, and I couldn't bear to go back into the house. Walking slowly around the yard, from garden to garden, bush to bush, tree to tree—I looked, felt, touched.

At first there was that quiet kind of reverence and then gradually I started gathering up sticks, tidying up and snapping off. I got a sack and a pair of scissors and started after the tulips that had been so breathtaking only a week before. Tut, tut. Here they were en masse, right in the front yard, stems pointing naked stamens into the air without their beautiful petal dresses. And next thing you know, they will have all of those yellowing leaves! What to do! Aha. I've seen gardeners who carefully fold tulip leaves over and fasten them with a rubber band. That way, they can be allowed to send the nutrients back down to the bulb and yet passersby aren't offended by their less than spectacular state of being, and gardeners, in turn, can have a continuously splendid looking garden.

I was just considering this tedious solution to my in-between garden, when I was overwhelmed with nature's metaphor. Nature doesn't work with on-off switches, or at continuously high RPMs. Nature is organic. It cycles, it flows. There is an ebb for every tide, a time of retreat and gathering of strength for every time of flowering. This continuous ebb and flow is vital in order to renew the energy required for a continuing cycle of life. And when it is interrupted, when the leaves are cut before they can become unsightly, the process is short-circuited. The bulb weakens and cannot produce the next season.

I sat down on the grass. Here was something for me. I have trouble with accepting the need for downtime. I want to be a continuous switch, a peak producer with no valleys. I want relationships that get better continuously; I want to make continuous improvement myself with no temporary backsliding. I want to be able to jump up the minute after I am kicked in the stomach. I just don't want to allow time to recover and take in strength. I want to be a non-stop flowering wonder. And I want every one else to be the same. No waiting around, no retreating, no fallow non-productive times.

And our expectations aren't just about human growth. We want companies that post continuous gains—every single quarter. We want countries that have been under totalitarian governments for decades to become smoothly functioning democracies in a matter of months. We elect officials and want them to change everything before the next election.

We want spiritual maturity, now. We want to be able to forgive immediately, to be submissive without a struggle, to understand without having to quietly study, ponder, and live.

I looked at the tulips. And then I looked at myself and this world. It doesn't make any sense. What are we thinking? Instant and relentless isn't the way of eternity.

I've always wondered about the phrase "long-suffering." At first glance it seems to indicate that being miserable for a long period of time is some kind of virtue to seek after. I don't think so! Then what could it mean? Perhaps "suffering" in this phrase could be interpreted to mean "allowing," as in "suffer the little children." Perhaps the Lord sees "allowing time, and allowing a long time" as a sorely needed virtue.

Could we allow time for our children to learn the lessons of life? Could we allow ourselves time to recover from periods of difficulty—time to grieve, time to heal, time to gather strength? Could we allow societies time to change and grow; businesses and ideas time to change and grow; individuals time to change and grow; relationships time to change and grow?

I looked at the tulip leaves again, beginning to yellow and wilt, and saw them differently. I can respectfully allow them some time. In fact, I can celebrate while I wait with them. My garden will gently call to those who walk by, "Pardon us, but good things are happening. We are gathering nourishment and preparing quietly for more glory."

ALTERNATIVES TO
GROWING OLD

Mary Ellen Edmunds

I don't remember when I first discovered I could
no longer "leap tall buildings in a single bound."
All of a sudden, there it was: The factoid of life regarding
MEE and tall buildings.

I also don't remember when I realized I could no longer
take the stairs two or three at a time . . . or hike Lady
Mountain in under two hours. I get winded now, just taking
the garbage can out to the street!

So I don't remember when I discovered that I was getting
older. Not old, really. Not yet. But older. Am I the same person
who was voted best female athlete in my high school? Is
this the body that could play just about any sport and jog
"forever" without getting tired?

Once when I was a student nurse at the LDS Hospital in
Salt Lake City, living in the nurse's residence on the corner
of Ninth Avenue and C Street, I had a clinic assignment

downtown. Having come from a small town, I didn't know how to use the bus system, so I just walked . . . all the way down and all the way back . . . up and down those hills . . . in my uniform (including the 2-pound white shoes!).

Those days are gone. And I never thought I'd be the one noticing these little acts of nature—these saggings and malfunctions and slowing downs and stuff. So I've been thinking about alternatives to growing old. I think a lot of it has to do with what I allow to go on inside of me. Here are some alternatives I've come up with. See what you think.

One was growing up, not old. I have considered that two or three times in my life, and I don't think I was meant to grow up. Some people just don't have what it takes.

Another alternative to growing old is growing happy. That's a good one. I like it.

As time goes on, I think our awareness improves, and we realize we're surrounded by reasons to be happy. I think we also become better "happifiers" to others as we collect a whole variety of experiences and memories.

Another option, probably related to growing happy, is growing content.

And growing more grateful.

Growing wise, and growing kind.

Growing endurable (I didn't say adorable, I said endurable). Maybe as we grow older we do grow more endurable—more capable of enduring to the end. Could it be that we can tell the end is getting closer? That's how the old movies used to finish (as if we couldn't tell on our own): "The End."

Isn't it wonderful that "The End" for our time as Earthlings will be "The Beginning" of the rest of forever? Likely we'll once again be leaping tall buildings in a single bound, and never growing old.

A LITTLE LESSON I LEARNED FROM CHOCOLATE

Emily Watts

The other day I had an important project at work that I simply had to make significant progress on. The first two hours of the day slipped past in a flurry of interruptions, as had the previous two full days. Finally, in desperation, I made a little sign for my office door that read: "If you have CHOCOLATE with you, come right in. Otherwise (unless you have a demonstrable emergency), you may wish to steer clear until the door opens."

I meant it as kind of a joke, really—a gentle hint that I needed some alone time. As it turned out, though, no fewer than five people showed up at my door with offerings of chocolate in the course of two hours. They didn't need anything from me; they just recognized my stress and wanted to help. It's made me think a little harder about the notion of "ask, and ye shall receive." Sometimes I think we're so determined to buck up and handle everything ourselves that we often cut ourselves off from sources of help—human and divine. We're too proud to ask.

I've often said, with no little irony, that I couldn't possibly have a cleaning service come in to my home because I'd have to do so much cleaning to prepare for them that by then I wouldn't feel the need. Silly, huh? But I think I do that spiritually, too—I want to get a handle on things, try to solve some of my problems myself, and then maybe I'll feel like I can let Christ into my life. It's so backwards! He knows about the mess already and is willing to step in and help anytime I'm willing to send up the signal to admit him.

I'm not perfect, but at least I'm getting better at admitting that, and at asking for the help I need. And whether it's chocolate or some other form of moral or spiritual support, I'm surely grateful for what I receive!

STOP, LOOK, AND LISTEN

Ardeth G. Kapp

It used to be that at every crossing next to the railroad track in my home town there was a large sign that read: Stop Look and Listen. The direction was very clear and in a particular order for a reason.

First, you were to stop. After complying with that simple directive you were to look, both ways, to see what might be coming down the track. And as if that weren't enough, to get a clear reading, you were also to listen.

In today's hurried world we may feel some days as though we are on a fast moving train along an endless railroad track. Perhaps it might be a good idea, foolish as it may sound, to mount a sign on our refrigerator door or some other conspicuous place: Stop Look and Listen.

Did you *stop* long enough to catch your breath and awaken your senses to the beauties of this season? Did you *look* at the blossoms forming on the trees before they were gone? Did you see the drenched and dripping apple tree after the rainstorm? Did you see the hand of God in all His creations for our enjoyment? Did you *listen* to the young birds as they returned to the feeders in the backyard that had been vacated for some time? When you listened, did you hear the sound of the magnolia warblers returning to your yard, which is also theirs?

Today may we stop long enough to give thanks to God for eyes to see, ears to hear, and life to live in this beautiful world.

HAPPY NEW YEAR!

Emily Watts

know the calendar suggests that New Year's Day is on January 1—and believe me, I appreciate the extra holiday so close to Christmas. My tree would probably be up until Easter otherwise. But for me, the day that really seems to signal a new year—or at least a new beginning—is September 1.

This is when we finally set aside the decadent summer chaos of midnight bedtimes and spontaneous weekend trips and avoidance of cooking and housekeeping. Delectable as all those things can be, they begin to wear on me, like too large a helping of chocolate cake (if, indeed, such a thing exists). I long for the plainer fare of schedules and structure.

September brings my life back into sane proportions. The kids are happily occupied in school, not yet overwhelmed with an accumulation of term projects, but productively engaged in getting the learning machine back into gear. Clean lockers, just-bought clothes, unspoiled notebooks, fresh boxes of colored pencils all the same length—these are the symbols of a new start for them.

Encouraged by their renewed resolve, I find myself looking for ways to bring greater accomplishments into my own life as well. This year, I want to work on being truer to what I know in my heart is right for me. This is partly due to the passing of Elder Maxwell and Elder Haight, which left me pondering, Have I been as faithful a disciple in my small sphere as they were in their larger one? Have I been as true to my life's mission as I might be? Recognizing that I have many worthy alternatives to choose from, am I making the best choices for this stage of my life?

One thing I've discovered is that today's best choice does not necessarily carry over into tomorrow. Circumstances change, and if I don't change with them I find myself feeling increasingly out of kilter. I just have to start over every now and then. This takes attention, prayer, and even some experimenting. That's why I'm grateful for an "extra" new year's day in September, a time to pull myself together and rethink some things and ask for guidance for the next leg of the journey.

So, although I'm not going to stay up until midnight to mark the occasion, may I wish you a very happy new year and another chance to make your life what you want it to be!

THE POWER TO FIND

James L. Ferrell

When our oldest child, Jacob, was very young, he used to hide things around the house. Unfortunately, one of those things was his mother's wedding ring. For months, he and his mother (Jackie) searched the house, trying to find where he had put it, with no luck.

Some time later, as Jackie and I were getting ready for our day, I couldn't find my hairbrush. I asked Jacob, then three and a half, if he had hidden it anywhere. He smiled, opened the cabinet door beneath the bathroom sink, and climbed in. A moment later, he backed his way out of the cupboard and handed me my brush.

"Jacob," Jackie exclaimed, "you're so good at finding things!"

"Yes," I agreed. "In fact, maybe you can find Mom's ring too."

Jacob grinned happily at us. "Okay, Daddy," he said. "And if I can't find it, I'll just pray to Heavenly Father and then Heavenly Father and Jesus will help me find it."

Jackie and I smiled at each other the way parents do when they are proud of the naiveté of their kids. *Such pure faith,* I thought to myself. *What a shame that he won't be able to find it.*

Jacob then walked out of the bathroom and opened the top drawer of Jackie's dresser—her jewelry drawer. He and Jackie had already been through that drawer at least five times. *Poor kid,* I thought. *You're not going to find it in there.*

The dresser stood taller than he was, so he was just reaching his little hand over the top edge of the drawer and feeling around for anything that felt like a ring. I patted his head as I walked passed him and out of the room. *Poor kid,* I thought to myself again.

From the landing outside of our room, I turned for one last look. There he was, still groping for anything in the drawer.

And then something happened that I will never forget. I watched as our little Jacob closed the drawer, folded his arms, and then prostrated himself face down on the floor to pray. *What pure, undefiled faith!* I thought. *What a shame that nothing will come of it,* I said, shaking my head. *I hope it doesn't shake him too much.*

After the prayer he immediately stood and opened the drawer. As before, he reached his hand over the top. Then, all of a sudden, he lifted it back out again. Between his index finger and thumb he was holding a ring. I was momentarily stunned. *No, it couldn't be,* I thought, as I started to walk toward him. *That would be impossible.*

Jacob surveyed what he was holding and then, with eyes shining and face radiant, announced, "Look, Daddy, I found the ring!"

And he had. But how could it be? We had emptied and searched that drawer so many times. What's more, he couldn't even see into it. Yet here was our humble boy, acting upon an impulse after a prayer of faith, holding aloft the ring I knew he would never find.

"I have the power to find, Daddy!" he said.

"Yes, son, you sure do," I agreed, wiping the tears out of my eyes and the disbelief out of my mind. "You do have the power to find."

He had the power to find, of course, because he had first found the Lord—someone I, obviously, had not found well enough.

Luckily, we are blessed with the faithful examples of children and others and with the words of the holy prophets, which declare the life and divinity of the Lord—the One who lives that we might find Him, and by finding Him, thereby find all.

GENUINE COMPLIMENTS

Mary Ellen Edmunds

I've been thinking about genuine compliments. That might sound redundant. As I read it again, it seems like we should be able to drop the "genuine"—that every single compliment we give should be real. From the heart. Genuine.

One reason I've been thinking a lot about compliments is because I think we don't share enough of them. We probably have zillions stored somewhere, and it's "high time" to start giving them away.

Let me give a little example and see if it reminds you of something. One Sunday in January of 2002, I noticed my neighbor Ben Hanks near the door of the chapel after our meetings had finished. He had just turned 16 a few months earlier. I had been meaning to talk to him, and I asked if he had a minute. I told him about Sunday, 08 December (five weeks or so earlier). I had wanted to have a meaningful experience partaking of the sacrament. I'd been thinking about it, praying about it, reading some scriptures and hymns, and hoping for a good experience.

I went to sacrament meeting early and once again began reading the words of hymns and some scriptures, doing what I could to help put myself in a position to have a very positive experience in partaking of the sacrament and renewing sacred covenants. I told Ben that I had sung the sacrament hymn, thinking carefully about the words, and then had closed my eyes and waited to listen intently to the words of the prayer. The priest began.

I said, "For some reason it seemed to me that the priest who was offering the prayer was going more slowly or more carefully, or both. He seemed to be thinking about what he was saying, and it didn't sound as though he was reading. It helped me so much!" I admitted that I had opened my eyes immediately following "amen" to see who had been the one to offer that prayer so beautifully.

"It was YOU, Ben." And then I thanked him sincerely for helping me to have what I had desired—a meaningful experience partaking of the sacrament that day.

Ben had been watching and listening intently. He said, "It was my first time, and I'd been thinking a lot about it. I wanted to do it right. I didn't want to just read what was on the card—I wanted it to be meaningful. I wanted to think about what I was saying." And then he added, "I wondered if anyone would notice. . . ."

Oh, my goodness. What if I hadn't noticed? Or what if I had noticed, but I hadn't said anything? Heavenly Father noticed, and He helped me notice, and He also prompted me to say something about it to Ben.

Is there someone who needs a genuine compliment from you? It could be a note or a phone call or anything that's possible for you in the midst of all else you're doing. Think about it. You might surprise someone right at the moment when they need it most.

HURRAH FOR FAMILIES!

Virginia Hinckley Pearce

We once had an interesting year for our family. Five of our six children had babies born within a nine-month period. During that same time my mother became ill and subsequently passed away. Being on the front lines of these six families as we dealt with the most profound events—birth and death—has been a sacred experience. I've learned and relearned many things, one of which I will attempt to explain.

Tolstoi said, "Happy families are all alike; every unhappy family is unhappy in its own way." I think I would like to take issue with him. You see, I have come away from this year believing that happy families are all incredibly and delightfully different. I have come away from this year with a renewed reverence for the family—the little nuclear family that is created by a man and a woman and their children. Together this little group of people blends their personalities, temperaments, talents, and quirky ways into an identity that is uniquely theirs—their own family culture.

There were many things about Mother's final illness and death that were sweet and even miraculous, but one of the sweetest parts for me was the two days following her passing when Dad and we five adult children worked together on the tasks that arise after a death. We went to the mortuary, we sat around the table and decided on a funeral program—who would do what, the music, and all of the details that go with those arrangements. Ever so quickly and with such easy grace, it was as if we turned the clock back and it was just the five of us with Mother and Dad in years that are long gone. Don't misunderstand me; we love every single spouse—our in-laws are wonderful people, and each has enriched and changed our family culture in happy ways. But there was something so natural about being just the five of us again as we made our plans to honor Mother. We all slipped back easily into our little family, like slipping into an old pair of sweats. It was so good!

The same reverential feelings came over me as I spent between one and two weeks helping out with each of our children's families as their babies were born. This time, I wasn't really even a participant in the family. I was just an observer. And every single family was different and unique in its reaction to the arrival of the new family member. What they all had in common was an almost giddy happiness.

We feel incredibly blessed to have six children who, as far as we know, are all striving to keep their covenants. One of the partners in each marriage grew up in our eccentric little home. Those are the things that are the same, but the similarities are fewer than the differences. I can tell you that every one of those families has developed its own culture. The things they do. The things they don't do. The things they fret about, the things they ignore. The routine of the household. The mood rhythms. The way they handle money and leisure time. The way they interact with each other and their children, etc. Some are more playful, some more serious, some focused and goal oriented, some casual and spontaneous.

But now, finally, here is the point of all this: I believe that there are so many ways to be a good and a happy family, and I worry that in our church we sometimes get too narrow. Some of us seem to think that all righteous families must follow the same family routine, they must all interact the same way, follow the same behavioral prescriptions. When mothers, particularly, hear of how someone else's family does it, we want to buy the pattern and impose it on our own, or we just settle for feeling "less than."

President Boyd K. Packer referred to this in October general conference: "I do not think it pleases the Lord when we worry because we think we never do enough or that what we do is never good enough" ("The Least of These," *Ensign*, Nov. 2004, 87).

Because of our father's prominence, the members of our

family are often asked very specific questions. "Tell us exactly what your father would say when . . . or exactly how did your mother get you to . . . " and on and on. It's hard to answer those questions and not feel a bit foolish. All of those things just developed because of the unique personalities of our parents—modified and changed by the unique personalities of their five children—and it all just happened! Culture is complicated. It isn't changed by a list of things we say or don't say, but is a result of patterns and interactions over time with some implicitly agreed upon commonalities. When those commonalities are the basic doctrines of the gospel, we are all free to fly and become uniquely happy.

C. S. Lewis said: "Sameness is to be found most among the most 'natural' men, not among those who surrender to Christ. How monotonously alike all the great tyrants and conquerors have been: how gloriously different are the saints" (*Mere Christianity*, Macmillan, 1943, 190).

If this is true for individuals, I believe it is also true of families.

When parents strive to keep their covenants, enabling the Spirit to work in their lives, every family will be wonderfully different. And we could be comparing less and celebrating more!

Hurrah for my family!

Hurrah for yours!

CALL HOME

Ardeth G. Kapp

few weeks ago, needing some information, I dialed a telephone number. I heard a recording giving me instructions: "For English, press one. For Spanish, press 2." Then I was asked several questions. Did I want billing, new service, reservations, and on and on. This was followed by: "If you wish to repeat this message press the pound key, if not press star or wait for an agent." And then, "There are four calls ahead of you."

On any given day you can get this response to a phone call: "You have reached the voice mail of John Doe. I am away from my desk right now, but if you wish to leave your number and a short a message I will return your call. Begin your message after the sound of the beep."

YES! I'd like to leave a message, I thought.

I want to talk to someone.

I want someone to listen.

I have a concern.

I want to be connected.

I need help.

But the phone goes dead. I hold it to my ear just waiting until a recording gives further direction. "If you want to make a call, please hang up and try again."

This world of "high tech" presents many challenges. And when we need answers, or at least need to be heard, how grateful I am that I can call "home" any hour of the day or night. I know someone who knows me, loves me, cares about me, and listens to me will hear and respond to my call. The communication lines are never down unless we break the line. And even then, the repair can be quickly made.

In the Bible Dictionary, we read: "As soon as we learn the true relationship in which we stand toward God (namely, God is our Father, and we are his children), then at once prayer becomes natural and instinctive on our part" (p. 752). It is so good to be able to call home. We can call in good times and in difficult times and know that He knows and understands. Help is always available.

THE EASTER POEM

Kathleen Hinckley Barnes Walker

*N*ephi records, "[The Lord] doeth not anything save it be for the benefit of the world; for he loveth the world, even that he layeth down his own life that he may draw all men unto him" (2 Nephi 26:24).

We were living in Denver when I turned five years old, and I was asked to recite an Easter poem in Jr. Sunday School on Easter Sunday. Because we were there on a temporary basis, our family resources of Church materials were almost nonexistent. There were no ward libraries or neighbors to borrow from, much less the Internet. So Mother, being ever resourceful, decided to write a poem. I dutifully memorized it and on that Easter Sunday, I stood up in my new little blue dress and white sandals and recited the following:

> *Some folks think that Easter time*
> *Is just for pretty clothes*
> *And Easter baskets filled with eggs*
> *Of colors bright and bold.*

But Mother told me differently—
It's for another reason.
For Jesus rose up from His tomb
That Happy Easter season.
This gives to me a precious gift,
It means that when I die,
I'll live again, as Jesus did,
And dwell with Him on high.

That message, learned so long ago, seemed to have res-onated with my little five-year-old spirit. "It means that when I die I'll live again, as Jesus did, and dwell with Him on high."

In the years since, I have often pondered this Easter thought. The story began on that obscure night when Jesus was born in Bethlehem. The years of His life unfolded and cli-maxed on that first Easter morn, when He overcame the bondage of death and arose from the grave in the magnificent resurrection. In that moment, the gift of eternal life was born for each of us.

As I read the events of that first Easter morning, I am touched by the great sense of loss and longing that was expe-rienced by those close to Jesus. He was their leader, their strength, and their Master. He had taught them and blessed them. They had witnessed His miracles and had felt His love. And now He had been wrongfully accused, brutally abused, and sadistically murdered by the evil designs and injustices of men. He was gone, and their loss was so great they could scarcely go on.

In the Gospel of John we read the account of Mary Magdalene, who, in the pre-dawn hours of that resurrection morning, went to the burial place of her Lord. In all probability she was seeking comfort, searching for solace amidst her deep grief. We can only imagine her feelings of darkness and despair when she found the stone rolled away and His body gone. I can see her standing and looking into the empty tomb. I can taste her tears as they rolled down her face. This loss seemed too much to ask anyone to bear, even Mary Magdalene, who had been the personal recipient of His miracles and who had lovingly followed and believed what Jesus taught. In that dark hour, she must have been weighed down by a great sense of loss and hopelessness.

And then, a miracle—an answer! For there appeared two angels, one standing at the head and the other at the feet, where the body of Jesus had lain. They said to her, "Woman, why weepest thou?" And she answered, "Because they have taken away my Lord, and I know not where they have laid him" (John 20:13). Just think of it! All she knew at that moment was that He was gone—really gone. The deep grief she must have felt is almost unimaginable.

She turned then to see Jesus standing before her. Her

despair was so consuming that she did not recognize Him when He asked, "Woman, why weepest thou?" Thinking He was the gardener, she responded, "Sir, if thou have borne him hence, tell me where thou hast laid him, and I will take him away" (John 20:15). Jesus Himself must have been touched by her great love for Him because as John records, He then spoke her name, saying, "Mary." At that instant the familiarity of His voice resonated and she answered, "Rabboni," which is to say, "Master" (v. 16).

It is hard to comprehend the tenderness of that moment.

As we think of our sister Mary Magdalene, we connect with her loss. We can feel her pain. Perhaps we have known her darkness. But we can also know, just as she came to know, that in our darkest hours the ministering angels bring comfort, and though they may not appear and speak to us as they did to Mary, yet they surround us and carry us and give peace to our aching hearts. We can understand, as Mary came to understand, that life goes beyond the grave. And though we have not seen our resurrected Lord, and we have not yet felt the nail prints in his hands and feet, we can know with certainty that He suffered and died and atoned for our sins, and more importantly, that He rose from the grave, providing us assurance of life eternal.

Yes, Mother told me differently—
It's for another reason.

For Jesus rose up from His tomb
That happy Easter season.
This gives to us a precious gift,
It means that when we die,
We'll live again, as Jesus did,
And dwell with Him on high.

SEASONS OF LIFE

Mary Ellen Edmunds

looked out the window and what did I see—popcorn popping on the apricot tree, covered with snow!

It's trying to turn into springtime in the Rockies, but it's taking a while. But I love the changing of the seasons. I like living where all four are distinctive. I like having the promise of the next one in the current one.

When I was a little kid, I loved summers, and my favorite months all had a *u* in them. Now I realize that things have changed. I've changed. All my favorite months now have an *r* in them.

Our lives have seasons, and perhaps, as with the weather, there are some seasons that seem more enjoyable, productive, interesting, beautiful, satisfying, or whatever. If our whole life were our favorite season, we likely wouldn't learn or grow as much. If my mother had allowed me to eat only my favorite food (macaroni and cheese) through all my growing-up years, I might have looked even worse today than I actually do!

Before my father "went home" (at age 95), I watched him go through many seasons. While some were exceedingly challenging, he seemed committed to doing his best no matter what his circumstance. Toward the end, I began having the feeling that he had been "seasoned to perfection." I've decided I love that phrase, and I hope as you think about it, it will make sense to you.

How about your life—what have your seasons been so far? We could narrow them down so that one of you out there who's about 50 could have had 100 seasons. If you have that much time to think, wow! Most of us will divide or group our years into fewer than 100 seasons.

Maybe you're in a season of raising children, doing your best to make sure they're happy and healthy, clothed and fed, bright and well-mannered, and so on. Do you receive a lot of advice about how to make it through this season? I hope you have more people to genuinely help than to just evaluate and judge what and how you're doing.

Maybe this is your season for a demanding Church calling, and if it were the ONLY thing you had to do in your life you could really "do a number" on it. But you're doing well—you're praying, studying, preparing, and giving your best. And you're somehow keeping up with all the other things in your life most of the time.

Maybe you're in a season of school, and you wonder if

you'll ever be finished with tests and papers to write and pages to read and lectures to comprehend. Do you think there will ever be a time when you can read for pleasure again?

Maybe your season is one of beginning your profession so that you can provide for you and your family. You've finished school (and it seems like it took half your life . . . because it did!), you've interviewed "all over the place," you've prayerfully considered what would be the best situation, and here you are, on your way.

Maybe this is a season for you as it is with my mother currently. She's 90 and realizes there are things she used to do which she just can't do any more. Is that your season too? (You don't have to be almost 90 before you realize there are things you can no longer do, eh?) She looks back on many interesting seasons—a mother of eight with many grandchildren and great-grandchildren, a nurse, Silver Beaver, self-taught farmer and vet, exceptional cook and gardener, Relief Society president, and so on. Your list is just as amazing.

Maybe you're in a season of missionary service, either as a young person or as someone who is considered a "senior missionary." For many, this particular season seems like an oasis. It's often so hard to say "yes" to promptings and invitations, but oh, the incredible experience of representing Jesus Christ wherever He sends you!

Maybe your current season is similar in some ways to

mine. (I don't know that we're ever in exactly the same circumstance as someone else.) I'm retired, but I'm as busy as I ever was. Inside I feel like I could still leap tall buildings, but in reality I can hardly leap into my socks.

I find myself humming "Have I done any good in the world today?" a little more often than I used to. I'm still looking forward most of the time, but I also find I look back more than I did when I was twenty or thirty. I'm never bored, and I feel thankful for that. I'm also deeply grateful that I tend to be happy and cheerful most of the time.

As I've been thinking about all of this, I've decided that many seasons overlap. Several might descend on us at once. We think spring has come, but there's another "cold snap." We think summer will be long and hot, and all of a sudden it's time to harvest the apples, roll up the hoses, and carve the pumpkins.

Ah, the seasons of our lives. Remember what I said about my dad? As he was ready to leave, I decided he was seasoned to perfection. What have your seasons taught you? Have they helped to bring insight, important memories, compassion, understanding, empathy, faith, perspective, patience, and many other qualities of soul? Are we getting all we can out of each of our seasons?

WHY I LOVE
THIS CHURCH

Emily Watts

My husband and I had a fabulous chance a few weeks ago to get away for two days alone together, so we left our two young teenagers in the hands of their 23-year-old brother and hopped a plane at 6:00 A.M. for the Pacific Northwest.

Turns out we forgot to communicate with Big Brother that he needed to go home after dropping us at the airport, so he could take his little sister to school. Alone in the house, she didn't wake up until 15 minutes before school was to start. She dressed in a panic, shouting for her brother to wake up, she needed a ride. Imagine that panic escalating in a 13-year-old's mind as she realized her brother wasn't there. Blissfully unaware, he had decided to get in an early temple session before his own classes.

When I heard about my daughter's solution to this problem, I cheered out loud: She called our home teacher. He told us later that she was hyperventilating by then, and he thought she was having some kind of medical emergency and dashed right over. He calmed her down, took her to school, wrote her a note to excuse her tardiness, and just generally took care of her.

I love that story because it shows me what home teaching is supposed to be. We're an active LDS family; I'm sure we could have been treated to the "drive-and-wave" approach to home teaching. But our home teachers come to our home every month. They speak individually with our children. They convey their caring, so much so that a 13-year-old girl knows where she can turn in a crisis. Our home teachers don't second-guess the program or the reasons for it, and as a result our lives have been blessed—not just in this instance, but in many ways over many years. We reap the benefits of their obedience.

This is what being willing to "bear one another's burdens" means to me. This is why I want to try harder to do everything I'm asked in the Church, even when I can't always see exactly why I'm being asked to do it. This is just another reason—in a whole crowd of reasons—why I'm grateful to be a Latter-day Saint.

THE MARVELOUS CYCLE
OF COMPLIMENTS

Hilary Weeks

I was in the grocery store a couple of weeks ago, and I was not having a very good day. I was feeling down. As I was shopping, a woman whom I did not know passed by me and said, "Your hair is really cute." Right in front of the cheese section, this woman single-handedly lifted my spirits. She liked my hair! I didn't even like my hair that day! Her kind compliment made me feel so good.

Compliments are wonderful little things. They do not cost anything, they take very little time, you never run out, and everybody likes them! (I wish I could cook a meal that had all those qualities.)

Have you ever noticed the marvelous cycle of goodwill that paying a compliment creates? When we compliment someone, they feel good. And we feel good because we noticed the good. Both the giver and the receiver are uplifted.

Dr. James M. Read, a doctor of psychology, says, "Take notice of praiseworthy situations and say something! Most of us don't get or give nearly enough genuine heart-felt compliments. The opportunities are all around. Catch your children being good . . . and heap on the attention and praise. Notice a stranger doing something kind . . . say something. Find a coworker going the second mile . . . don't let it go uncelebrated."

The Savior was a wonderful example of giving genuine compliments. When Mary Magdalene stood outside the empty tomb, the Savior appeared and said to her, "Woman, why weepest thou?" (John 20:15). I am intrigued by the term "woman"—it is not one that we use much today. But in the Savior's day the term "woman" was so respectful that it was reserved to address the most regal of women. That the Savior called Mary Magdalene by that name was a compliment. He also referred to His mother by that name (see John 19:26). They were most definitely queenly women, deserving of such respect.

I find it even more inspiring and tender to note that He addressed the woman caught in adultery by that same term. When she was brought before Him, He showed her that very same divine love and respect. I wonder how she felt at that moment. Surely she viewed herself differently because of the respect He paid her (see John 8:10).

Compliments lift us all. They are like helium for our self-esteem and are one of those "small and simple things" that help "great things come to pass."

So go ahead, give as many compliments as you want to give today!

MY FAMILY MIRACLE!

Carolyn J. Rasmus

Along with many other ward members, I responded to our bishop's challenge to find two family names and prepare the necessary work so that the ordinances could be performed in the temple.

Several years prior, I had gathered information on ancestors from my mother's line but had never entered the work or prepared the names for temple ordinances. So, acting on my bishop's challenge, I pulled out old files and went to work. There were more than 200 names, and I determined to submit all of these names so our ward would have ample opportunities to participate in temple ordinances.

For some unknown reason, I had done little research on my father's line. Shortly after joining the Church in 1971, I was anxious to complete my four-generation chart. I had no difficulty finding four generations on my mother's side of the family, but I knew little of my father's family. His father had died when Dad was only thirteen years of age, and all my father knew of my grandpa was that he had come from

Germany. I wanted to know the exact location, but even church and civil records listed only Germany.

Finally, on a trip to my home in Ohio, my dad took me to visit his sister. "Aunt Helen keeps a lot of records," he said. Aunt Helen had many obituaries and notes, but the only records about her father indicated that he had been born in Germany. Finally, she suggested that an old blacksmith in town might know their father's birthplace since he had known the Rasmus family in Germany.

We went to see the man that afternoon. Though I do not remember the name of the blacksmith, I have vivid recollections of the dirt in the shop and on the blacksmith. This older man had lost much of his hearing and had no teeth. My father yelled to identify himself and finally asked, "Do you know where in Germany my father was born?" The blacksmith responded with one word, which I didn't understand, but my father said immediately, "Fehmarn! That's it! I remember my father saying he was born on an island by the name of Fehmarn."

I could hardly wait to return to Utah and visit the Family History Library. With the help of a research assistant I located Fehmarn, an island only eight by twelve miles, located in the Baltic Sea—as close to Denmark as to Germany. The researcher provided me with a form letter in German and suggested I send it to the pastor of the Lutheran Church in the largest town on the island. I was excited and ecstatic! But the researcher told me this was like looking for a needle in a haystack and that I might never receive an answer to my inquiry. Undaunted, I mailed the materials, and in less than three weeks I had received hand-copied records for the births, marriages, and deaths of four generations!! This was truly a miracle. I wrote to the pastor, thanking him for his help and asking for information on the families of these ancestors. He again responded with the information requested.

All of the temple work was completed for these people and then in the busyness of life, I put things away and did nothing more. Even as I began preparing names for this current project, I left untouched any of the Rasmus line.

Then one Sunday evening, I happened to glance at my Grandfather Rasmus's family group sheet. I noticed that the town of birth was spelled differently in two places. But since I wasn't working on this line, I determined I'd fix it later. But for some reason, I kept thinking of this error. Finally, I went into the Internet to learn the correct spelling of this small town. I noticed there was a map of the island and several other links that seemed they might contain more information about this island.

Then, without knowing how I arrived at this link, I was looking at a site labeled, "Genealogical Society of Fehmarn." I quickly explored this Website and found that to gain full access to the material it was necessary to give evidence that one's ancestors came from this island. I immediately sent an e-mail to the Webmaster, indicating the names and vital information of my ancestors. Within fifteen minutes, I received a return e-mail giving me access to the names and a paragraph in red letters, informing me that I would be pleased with the information about my family.

I could hardly believe my eyes! There, on my computer screen, appeared generation after generation of ancestors—all arranged in family group sheets and on a pedigree chart! Some lines went back to the year 1511 and represented fifteen generations of relatives!

The circumstances of my finding this site convinced me that I was being lead by the Lord and touched by the Spirit of Elijah. I felt an obligation to respond with promptness. Within days, I was able to take the names of these ancestors to the local Family History Library and have the names readied for their ordinance work to be performed in the temple: 945 ordinances for women; 1,087 ordinances for men; and the sealing of 97 couples.

I am so grateful for a bishop who was inspired to challenge each of us to find two ancestors for whom we could do temple work. I'm grateful for the promptings of the Holy Ghost, which drew my attention to the misspelling of a town name, and for the guidance of the Lord which lead me to hundreds of ancestors.

What a blessing to live in a time when sacred, saving ordinances can be performed in the House of the Lord for our departed ancestors! Truly my heart has been turned to my fathers, and I'm grateful for the opportunity to assist in performing the temple ordinances for my newly found relatives and becoming part of an enormous eternal family. Think of the reunion we are going to have!

A thought provoking postscript: That good blacksmith in Ohio passed away just six months after I met him and received from him that vital information, which enabled me to find my relatives.

WHEN I RUN OUT OF BIRTHDAYS

Ardeth G. Kapp

had gone to Tucson, Arizona, to spend a few wonderful and memorable days with my niece Shelly as she gave birth to her fourth little boy. Prior to delivery, three young boys waited anxiously for the arrival of their little brother who was making the transition from his heavenly home to begin his experience on earth. Now, he had joined them, and each little brother took turns reverently cradling this tiny baby in his arms for a time. It seemed to me as though they already knew him in an interesting way.

Soon after this moment of reverence and celebration, I was sitting at the kitchen table with these young children, painting rocks, making birds and fish and bugs and other creative possibilities. Six-year-old Josh, holding his paint brush and looking very serious, asked the question: "How many birthdays do you have left Nana Ardie?"

I smiled and asked, "What do you mean, Josh?"

He reached out his arms to give me a hug and said, "I love you, and I don't want you to ever die."

At that moment, the reality of mortality and immortality swept through my mind like a glorious drama in which we all take part. We enter this life as a baby and, in what seems like so few birthdays, there comes a time for us to return. We each have our time on stage.

With my arm around this little blond-headed boy and realizing that Easter was upon us, I said, "Josh, I have something wonderful to tell you. I don't know how many birthdays I have left, but that part doesn't really matter. What really matters is to know that Jesus came to this earth like your little baby brother. He did what he came to do. Then he died and was resurrected. Because of his great love for each of us, he made it possible that there would never be an end to our love for each other. Just like when I say good-bye to you and go back to Utah, we still keep loving each other and look forward to seeing each other again. When I run out of birthdays, I will go back home, but we will still keep loving each other and look forward to when we will be together again."

He smiled, and as he went back to painting his rock there came into my mind the words of Helaman to his sons, "And now, my sons, remember, remember that it is upon the rock of our Redeemer, who is Christ, the Son of God, that ye must build your foundation . . ." (Helaman 5:12).

SOMEDAY

Emily Watts

My baby is having a baby.

It's a girl, we found out recently, which was what I was secretly hoping—maybe because my oldest was a girl. It just seems a fitting completion of the cycle.

Now I'm really going to have to rein in my husband, who has for years been bringing into stock all manner of toys and books "for the grandbabies." (What use the grandbabies will have in the next decade or so for the radio-controlled tanks that let off a puff of smoke when attacked is a little beyond me, but I guess it doesn't hurt to be prepared.) Now that the time is imminent and the gender is known, I don't know how he'll restrain himself.

I remember thinking years ago that I would be a grandmother someday. What astonishes me—although it shouldn't, with all the times I've experienced it—is how quickly "someday" comes. One minute you're leading your kindergartner into his new classroom at the elementary school, and the next minute you're waving him through the door at the Missionary

Training Center. The weird thing is, while he was in kindergarten, it seemed like forever, and now that it's past it seems like it hardly took any time at all.

Maybe that's why the Lord told Joseph Smith that his afflictions would be "but a small moment" (D&C 121:7). If looking back from the perspective of a few years can have that kind of time-warp effect, imagine what seeing things from an eternal perspective could do!

My baby is having a baby. The cycle completes itself and begins again, as it has for generations and will for generations to come. With all of the "somedays" that have come and gone, the shining thread of that eternal pattern weaves through everything. Before we blink again, a lifetime of small moments will have spun itself into a family to last for eternity.

AFTER WE PUT
CHRISTMAS AWAY

Dean Hughes

January is such a great month. It feels downright stimulating to lay off the rich foods, clear the sugar from our veins, work up a sweat on the old stationary bicycle—and feel so righteous about it.

January is also that wonderful time when I've worn out my desire to go to the mall ever again. Every day that I don't charge a penny on my credit card, I feel like I'm bringing a healthy balance back to my life—and checkbook. (So much joy for doing so little!)

It's that dark, cold time of the year (at least in the Northern Hemisphere), when we may feel some cabin fever, but sleep comes so naturally. It's great to go to bed a little earlier, turn on the electric blanket, and curl up like a big old bear. (We've even stored up the extra fat to sustain us through our hibernation.)

I just hope, as we throw out the dried-up Christmas tree

and store away all our decorations, that we don't put away Christmas entirely—that is, the best part of Christmas. We seem to care more for others during the holidays and make a special effort to express those feelings with our cards, our greetings, our donations to those who are not as blessed as we are. And then, for some reason, we act almost as though those expressions were part of our over-indulgence, and we seem to withdraw to a spirit that isn't nearly so generous.

It almost seems as though we're a little embarrassed now, in the cold of winter, for all that warmth we shared. Do we think it got a little too cheesy, a little too over the top? What if we took a treat—a healthy one—to all our neighbors now, or in April or September? Would people think we had gotten all weird on them or something? How did we get started with the idea that we should be what we really ought to be in December and then pull back and wait again for eleven months?

I remember a United Way director who said that Americans love to buy a turkey for a single mom with kids at Thanksgiving or Christmas, even though she would be helped much more by a case of peanut butter in August—and that's when no one thinks about her. Interesting.

"O Little Town of Bethlehem, How still we see thee lie. Above thy deep and dreamless sleep, the silent . . ."

It sounded good, didn't it? When I was a bishop, I once

had our chorister do all Christmas songs during a sacrament meeting in July. I told our members that we always say that we want to keep the spirit of Christmas with us all year, but we don't work very hard to do it. The songs were just a little reminder. Maybe we should sing them all year.

To celebrate Christ's birthday, we eat too much and spend too much, and we feel guilty about it. It feels good to return to some austerity. We vow not to get so carried away next year. Suppose we actually did that? Suppose we cut back on some of the eating and spending next year but began right now to spread out the spiritual side of Christmas to every month of our year? It may sound a little too idealistic, but don't we actually know people who do just that? The fact is, there are those around us who need us every month of the year, and we need them. We also need Christ—his Spirit—with us, always. I think this should be the year we make some changes.

Let's do this year right, and then make next Christmas the fitting conclusion to a year full of kindness and generosity. I'm serious. We can do it.

GREAT FAITH HAS A SHORT SHELF LIFE

Kim A. Nelson

Elder Henry B. Eyring of the Quorum of the Twelve Apostles made this comment in response to President Hinckley's invitation to the Church to read the Book of Mormon: "I have built a great reservoir of faith by starting early and being steady in obedience. I will store it away against the times when I will be tested in storms. . . . because great faith has a short shelf life" ("Spiritual Preparedness: Start Early and Be Steady," *Ensign*, Nov. 2005, 39).

The insightful observation that "great faith has a short shelf life" reminded me of one of the Savior's parables—and storms—in my own life. I took a trip one Thanksgiving many years ago with my wife, Lois, to visit her grandfather in Butte, Montana. We were in college at the time and had a new baby daughter who had never met her great-grandpa. We drove home during a huge snowstorm, one of the worst I can remember. There were hundreds of cars off the road.

On a dark stretch of very lonely road I looked down and realized that we were almost out of gas. I am sure many of us have had the experience of watching the gas gauge fall and beginning to worry. The tension builds as we realize we are running on fumes. On that snowy night I found myself on an unfamiliar stretch of road, responsible for a young wife and a new baby. I really didn't know how far it was to the next gas station. It's not enough to say that at that moment I wished I had paid more attention to my fuel.

The truthfulness of what Elder Eyring taught, "great faith has a short shelf life," became more evident to me as I remembered the panicked feeling of watching the needle drop. Because we don't know when a storm is coming, or how long it might last, we must top off our spiritual tanks whenever we can. Frequent spiritual refills will allow us to be better prepared for those unfamiliar stretches of dark road and the storms that will surely come.

It is ample spiritual fuel that provides us with the power to safely go the distance.

FOOD FOR THOUGHT

Hilary Weeks

I have always loved to clean. Even as a teenager, I kept my room clean. (It's true; you can ask my mom.) A clean environment allows me to clear my mind and focus on what I am working on. You know the feeling—it is just cozy!

One night, when I was a student at BYU, all my roommates were gone, so I tidied up the kitchen. It sparkled. Then I lit a candle and dimmed the lights to create the perfect ambiance. I remember looking forward to having a home of my own someday in which to create that same feeling.

Well, I do have a home of my own now, and guess what? I still love to clean! I am sure I drive my children a little crazy sometimes, but I am trying to teach them to value the pleasures and advantages of having a clean home.

A few years ago, I read an article where the writer described his mind as a park. A beautiful park with flowers, trees, a pond—even a bench to sit on. When an inappropriate thought entered his mind, or "park," he imagined litter appearing. The litter polluted his beautiful park, and he immediately removed it.

I adopted that idea because I could relate to it. Instead of a park, I picture in my mind a beautiful home—in perfect order (even fresh vacuum marks!). When I have a thought that should not be there, I picture junk being dumped in my "home." I imagine the room becoming cluttered, and I chase the thought away to restore cleanliness.

President Boyd K. Packer said, "Thoughts are talks we hold with ourselves. Do you see why the scriptures tell us to 'let virtue garnish [thy] thoughts unceasingly' and promise us that if we do, our 'confidence [shall] wax strong in the presence of God; and the doctrine of the priesthood shall distil upon [our] soul[s] as the dews from heaven' and then 'the Holy Ghost shall be [our] constant companion'?"

As we think about positive, uplifting things, those thoughts permeate our souls and we become more positive.

On occasion I have allowed my thoughts to make me feel guilty. I am grateful for this additional insight from President Packer. "Sometimes guilt controls our minds and takes us prisoner in our thoughts. How foolish to remain in prison when the door stands open."

Louisa May Alcott was only fourteen when she wrote these lines:

A little kingdom I possess,
Where thoughts and feelings dwell,
And very hard I find the task
Of governing it well; . . .
I do not ask for any crown
But that which all may win,
Nor seek to conquer any world
Except the one within.

Let the Spirit guide your thoughts. Pray for something good to ponder. Think about a scripture you recently read. Keep a quote of the day in your pocket on a small piece of paper. Refer to it throughout the day. Put a penny in your shoe. When you step on it, think something good about someone in your family.

Allow your thoughts to beautify the "home" or "park" in your mind. Such small things; but they play a huge role in who we become. Just a little food for thought.

(Quotes taken from President Packer, "The Spirit of Revelation," *Ensign*, Nov. 1999, 23.)

GETTING RID OF JUNK

Cherie Call

'm having my first baby in a few months, and
already there are a lot of changes happening
around our house. My husband and I are very busy people,
and I have to admit that whenever we've had spare moments
to clean, it's mostly involved the normal wiping, vacuuming,
and tidying. Lately, though, we've been thinking about the
tiny lungs of our new baby, and we've started washing walls
and inspecting every nook and cranny of our house.

We spend quite a bit of time on each room, and there are
a couple of rooms we haven't hit yet. One of them is the room
I dread the most. It's the most horrible room in the house. It's
also the room that will eventually become the baby's room.
It's my office.

Before Joe and I got married, he owned a house and had
roommates. When we got married, though, naturally the
roommates were kicked out, leaving us with a couple extra
rooms. These became offices—one for Joe and one for me.

Now before you start crying out at how unfair it is that

I'm the one losing my office, let me tell you that I truly deserve to lose this office. First of all, I'm just not really an office-y person when it comes to my work as a songwriter. I do most of my songwriting lying on a couch with my notebook or curled up in all sorts of locations in the house with my guitar.

I had high hopes of being more of a fancy office person when I first moved in. I hung lots of inspirational pictures and quotes on the walls, we put in a huge desk, and I even hung posters of some of my favorite songwriters. It was perfect.

But pretty soon some other piles started making homes there. Like when the home teachers were coming over and I still had a huge stack of mail on the kitchen table, I'd whisk it away to the office. Or a sewing project I never quite finished. Or stacks of CDs I had been using for things that I didn't have time to re-file. You get the idea. The piles grew and grew and I'm embarrassed to even try to describe what it looks like now.

For several months I could just shut the door and make everything disappear. I'd go days without worrying about it. But pretty soon there will not be room for my laziness. I know that a tiny, beautiful human being will need that room. I think about it every day. When I feel overwhelmed by it, I try to think of what a perfect room it will be when there are clean drawers filled with tiny, fresh smelling, soft clothing and blankets. I think of how fun it will be to paint the walls. I think of what it will be like to bring home that little child and to gently lay her down in a sparkling clean, cozy, peaceful haven.

A lot of people have told me that having kids will change my life. Some people speak of this in a negative way. I hear, "You won't matter anymore. You won't be allowed to care about yourself or let others care about you anymore. You'll be second place. You'll have to quit doing all the things you love."

Some other women tell me different, more incredible, positive things, though. They say, "You'll become braver. Things that would have frightened you before will not make you afraid, when you're the one who has to protect your children."

When I first heard this, I thought they might be talking about stepping on spiders. I remember being amazed at how my mom could fearlessly get rid of the nastiest of spiders and bugs and how I felt I could never do it. I felt the same awe when I saw her deal with some pretty nasty bathroom emergencies.

I think I've been the most amazed and inspired by a story one of my good friends told me the other day. She told me that she used to live in a very dangerous neighborhood. One night there was a gang shootout happening right outside her door. She crouched down under a window while it was happening. But she wasn't cowering in fear. She was making sure all of her kids were staying down, and she was peeking through the blinds, writing down license plate numbers! When I asked her how she could be so brave, she said, "I had no choice. I'm a mom."

I hope I am never in that situation myself. I wonder if I could really be that brave. But I like the idea of motherhood making me stronger and braver than I am now. I feel like I'll actually matter much more than I have before because I'll be giving such a huge piece of myself to the people I love. I'm so excited to be a mom. I consider it to be an honor. Maybe it's naïve, but I'm not really too worried about all the other things people tell me. Having a family has been a lifelong dream for me. It's what life is all about.

So, the least I can do is clean a messy room. I know this is not a new analogy, but this is hitting home with me right now. Maybe we all have some kind of messy room in our life somewhere. Maybe it's taking up emotional space we could give to our family members. Or maybe it's even keeping us from being closer to the Savior. I try to hide the messy pieces of my life, but those are the very places that Jesus needs to see. I want to be able to open every door and window of my soul, with no shame, for the world to see. I can't do that without the Savior's help. So as silly as it may seem, I think I'm going to say a little prayer right now, get out a huge garbage bag, and get to work.

STAYING CONNECTED

Ardeth G. Kapp

Years ago the only telephone service that was available in my hometown, for those that could afford a telephone, was one black telephone centrally located in the hall of the house with a 25-foot cord that could be taken from one room to the next as far as the cord would reach. It was considered a luxury if you were one of the few who had a four-party line instead of a ten-party line. A private line was a thing of the future. This meant that each family on a ten-party line would be sharing the line with nine other families, and each would have a distinctive ring. Our number was 3, and the ring was two longs and a short. A call could be picked up by any of the other nine parties when they would hear our ring. The only thing that afforded any privacy was the courtesy of the other members on the line to not pick up the phone unless it was their specific ring. It was well-known that curiosity often overcame courtesy, but that was not all bad. In fact there were some significant advantages, providing you wanted to get your message carried far and wide—as far and wide as the boundaries of our little village.

My Grandpa Leavitt arranged with the Alberta Telephone Company to have the equipment, the "switchboard" that would serve our town, installed in one of the front rooms of my grandparents' home in a booth located just inside the front entrance to the house. Grandma Leavitt hired and trained the switchboard operators, who worked six days a week from 8:00 A.M. to 6:00 P.M. Outside those hours, the lines were dead. If there ever were an emergency before or after those hours, a loud ring would sound throughout the whole house and would be answered immediately. But otherwise, the telephone office with the switchboard was closed and silent, which meant no telephone service to the town.

When Grandma was training the new operators, my cousin Colleen and I were very attentive. It was exciting to see how you could plug a cord with a metal tip into a hole on the switch board connecting one family, plug in another for another family, then turn a little crank that would ring in both homes and they would be connected.

One time, my cousin and I took it upon ourselves to try to solve a real town crisis. You see, a boy in our school several grades ahead of us really liked a girl who really liked him. For some unknown reason, they had refused to talk to each other ever again unless the other spoke first. All the kids in town were aware of the situation, and everyone tried to persuade either one to approach the other. But each refused to break the silence. This went on for days, and we all shared in the concern for this broken friendship.

On a Sunday afternoon, with a secret plan, my cousin and I took it upon ourselves to heal this friendship. We knew we had a great idea. We crept into the telephone office that was supposed to be closed, climbed up on the stool that the operator used, plugged in one cord, rang the bell, and when Billy answered the phone I said in a very grownup, official voice, "Just a minute, please."

Then we plugged a cord into the hole that would connect so we could ring his girlfriend's number. When she answered, my cousin said, "Go ahead, please," in the same tone the operators used. We were each wearing a headset and stood smiling from ear to ear as we listened in on the conversation. First from Becky, "Oh, I'm so glad you called."

"I didn't call you, you called me."

"No I didn't. You called me. I came to the phone and you were on the line."

"No, my phone rang, I picked it up and you were on the line."

There was a long pause.

"Then how did it happen?" one of them asked.

The ice had melted. We heard laughter, and once we

knew they were talking to each other, we pulled both plugs and cut short their conversation. The next day at school everyone was discussing "the mystery of the healed friendship" and wondering how it happened. Colleen and I kept it a secret for years.

Today we have wonderful new technology not like the old-time telephone with the operators you could speak with. We have computers, e-mail, voice mail, and phones, even cell phones where you can just hear a recording and leave a message. I sometimes wonder if that is an entirely good thing. If friendship is to survive and be strengthened, there must be a connection—communication that keeps friends in touch by talking one to another, preferably face to face.

LANE ENDS, MERGE LEFT

Hilary Weeks

$\mathcal{I}$ have a somewhat strange little tradition. I have absolutely no recollection of when or why this "ritual" started . . . but, every time I see a Frito-Lay truck, I think to myself, "Everything is going to be okay." Surely there is some logical and intelligent explanation of its origin. I have some faint memory of it being a funny experience. Nevertheless, a Frito-Lay truck brings a smile to my face and a simple, reassuring thought to my mind.

Funny how something common, transposed by creativity becomes meaningful. It is still the same thing, you just choose to see it differently.

Before you read any further, I need to tell you that this exercise requires a few minutes of your time and a little participation. If now is not a good time, come back when the kitchen is tidy, the kids are settled, and you have a few minutes of uninterrupted time. No, wait, who knows when that will be. Maybe now is as good a time as any!

This won't be hard—I think it will actually be fun. First,

look over the common roadside signs listed below. Then, pick three or four that jump out to you or pique your interest:

Stop	No Outlet
Wrong Way	Dead End
Yield	Slow, Children at Play
Keep Right	Service Vehicles Only
One Way	No Pedestrian Traffic
No U-Turn	Construction Ahead
Speed Limit	Work Area Ahead
Do Not Pass	Surface May Be Icy
Detour	Slow, Proceed with Caution
Road Closed	Stop, Do Not Enter

Now, turn the three or four you've chosen into an object lesson. Create an object lesson or phrase that means something to you personally. Let it relate to your current circumstances. Perhaps it could remind you of something important. Maybe it could be something that makes you giggle or brings a smile to your face.

For example: STOP. "Stop worrying about the things you can't control." Or, "Stop after one helping of apple pie." Or, "Stop all self-defeating thoughts."

Go ahead. Give it a try . . .

I wish I could read some of the ideas you came up with!

We see road signs every day. Why not turn them into quick, positive reminders! The negatives are already plentiful. This could be our way of adding more positives!

Just in case you'd like a few more ideas, here are some additional "object phrases."

Speed Limit: Someone give me a ticket because I am speeding through life! There is a limit to how fast I can go each day. It's okay to slow down.

Detour: What am I allowing to detour me from doing the important things?

Slow, Children at Play: Slow down and play with the children!

Yield: Yield to the promptings of the Spirit.

One Way: One way I can teach my children is by example.

No Pedestrian Traffic: I need a little time to myself, so no disturbances for the next couple of minutes!

No Outlet: Oh yes there is! Repentance!

Surface may be icy: On the outside one may seem cold or aloof, but on the inside they want to be warmed by love.

Construction ahead: . . . And it's going to make me better and stronger than I was before.

"How true it is that what we really see day by day depends less on the objects and scenes before our eyes than on the eye themselves and the minds and heart that use them." —F. D. Huntington.

WHICH WAY IS RIGHT?

Emily Watts

A couple of weeks ago, my husband and I got to travel to Maine and Massachusetts for several days to see the sights and spend time with some of our favorite cousins. As we were reflecting together about the experience on our flight home, we were struck by the fact that the two households in which we had stayed were on opposite ends of the spectrum in so many ways. The first was in rural Maine, which was green and lush and beautiful and woodsy and remote. We had to drive miles to get anywhere, and we took a mostly solitary tromp along the coastline and out across a "breakwater" (essentially a large stone wall) to get to a lighthouse.

In Boston, we were constantly surrounded by people. Our tromping this time took us along the "Freedom Trail," a sequence of historic landmarks including the graveyard where John Hancock is buried and the church from which the lanterns signaled the British invasion, "One if by land, two if by sea." The fascinating thing was that these sites just poked up in assorted spots throughout downtown Boston, surrounded by modern buildings and by people going about their everyday business. We got there on a crowded subway and didn't even need a car to get to most places that interested us.

The two families we stayed with were also quite different. I adore my cousin in Maine, who cooks and knits and quilts and hangs out with her grandchildren and grows a wonderful vegetable garden from which we ate hand-picked asparagus. And I adore my cousin in Massachusetts, who teaches high-school physics and supports six children in a staggering variety of activities and is more fun to talk to than just about anyone on the planet. They both have great marriages. They both have great families. They are both committed, loving Latter-day Saint mothers who serve in the Church and attend the temple and share their devotion to Heavenly Father by living with open, generous hearts.

That experience taught me, once again, that there are lots of right ways to "do life" if the fundamental principles are in place. If the foundation is strong, the architecture can vary widely and be wonderful in all kinds of iterations. I'm convinced that it is not our list of accomplishments but the condition of our hearts that will determine our standing when we come before the Savior to be judged. And I'm grateful to know, from my own observation, that He loves all kinds of women!

PORCHES

Mary Ellen Edmunds

*I*f we were together, I'd ask you to sing with me. When I tell you the words at the beginning of the song, I think you might catch on to the tune:

"Where have all the porches gone?" And so on.

For years I've had this thing on my mind about porches. When I walk in the mornings, I notice them. I also notice their absence.

This is one of the things that seems to have changed with the speed and pace of our lives.

When I was growing up, it seemed that more homes had porches, and more people used them. I loved it when the Palmers would be out on the porch, maybe with Roland playing his guitar and singing "Hallelujah, I'm a bum. . . ." (I'm not kidding!)

I loved it that Joneses were out on their porch as I'd roller skate by (although I didn't appreciate it when they laughed when I'd crash).

I love Kent and Karen's porch in Draper with the big,

comfortable swinging bench (what's the "real" name for those wonderful inventions?). There's a big tree near for shade.

Sometimes my neighbor Fran sits out on her small porch in the evening, and pretty soon others gather. I hope she'll do that again this year when it gets a little cooler.

Other neighbors will line up chairs along the front of their home, and anyone is welcome to stop by and sit and visit for a while. Almost like a porch extension, with a friendly, welcoming feeling.

I think we'd all be better off if there were more porches and if we used them frequently. We'd be more in touch with each other. Porches bring people together.

Do you have a porch? Or could you just put some chairs out in the front yard? A porch doesn't need to be fancy. In fact, it seems that some of the porches on brand new homes might only be there for decoration—some look like they've never been used. I think some aren't even wide enough for a chair.

Maybe you live in an apartment on the 15th floor, and it might be dangerous to try to put chairs out there on that little balcony thing. But where it's possible, could you create a porch-like feeling? Maybe someone could play a guitar or harmonica once in a while. Maybe you'd even like to sing.

I love doing that with friends and family—gathering and singing the familiar songs and visiting. Even without a campfire. Solving world problems. Sharing burdens and joys. Sitting quietly. Just being together.

I once heard a family described as "world-class porch sitters." I love the sound and feel of that. If you live in a neighborhood where there are several porches, you could form a porch association. Nothing formal with dues and rules . . . just a fun way to encourage each other and act organized.

I've got a little porch (room for one at a time unless you need to open the door). I think I'm suffering from porchlessness. Do you feel that way ever?

I'm thinking of saving my pennies and expanding out toward the driveway and having a real porch. (But first I need to get hearing aids).

Ask me about it the next time you see me. And think about doing something that will create a porch-like feeling where you live.

GOT ENERGY?

Hilary Weeks

We used to live in Colorado. There was a restaurant near our home that had a country store in the lobby. One evening as we waited for a table, I browsed around the store and came across a section of plaques with quotes hanging on the wall. One in particular cracked me up. It read, "I don't repeat gossip . . . so listen closely."

You might be wondering, "What does this quote about gossip have to do with wanting more energy?"

I constantly find myself wishing I had more energy. It seems wasted on the young. My one-year-old is like a mini-tornado ripping through my house. She gets into everything—drawers, cupboards, closets, etc. And I'm the disaster relief crew picking up the rubble every twenty minutes. Of course, that is just the tip of the responsibility iceberg! I need more energy!

Fortunately, the Doctrine and Covenants offers some insight on how we can invigorate our minds and bodies.

Section 88, verses 124 and 125, suggest some very sensible things:

- Don't be idle or lazy
- Keep yourself clean
- Go to bed early and wake up early
- Don't sleep longer than you need
- Don't find fault with others

Whoa! I wasn't aware that finding fault with others can drain my energy as much as not getting to bed early enough. When I read that verse, it hit me like a ton of bricks. I can't afford to find fault with others—doing so would prevent my mind and body from being invigorated! (Not to mention the fact that the Savior taught us otherwise.)

I used to visit teach an amazing woman named Gayle Stock. She radiated light and joy. She always made me feel as though our visits were the most important part of her day. I enjoyed every minute with her. During one visit she shared the following story:

As a young woman, her mother had been invited to a friend's home to play. As they sat on the friend's bed, the girl-friend began to gossip about one of their other friends. She tried to get Gayle's mom to do the same. Though the friend persisted, Gayle's mom refused to make any negative comments about their friend. A few minutes later, the friend they were gossiping about revealed herself. She had been hiding in the closet, listening to their conversation.

I have often wondered what I would have done in that situation.

I have found that when I look for the good in others, I love them more. There is another unexpected side effect—we also learn to love ourselves more.

Well, there has probably been a small microburst somewhere in my house. I guess I've got some toys to go clean up . . .

THE LITTLE THINGS

Merrilee Boyack

spend a lot of time saying little prayers of thanks. I am grateful for the weirdest, small stuff. It makes life interesting. Maybe I'll share a few.

I am grateful for the guy who invented Post-It Notes. OK, maybe it was a woman—or maybe a committee. Bless them. I write the odd things I need to remember to buy on those wonderful notes and slap them on my chest. Then when I go to the grocery store, the clerk turns her head to read my chest and says, "Did you remember the sour cream?" Often I have forgotten. So bless them. I'm grateful.

And those "flag" critters—the skinny Post-It Notes—are killer. Now I mark all the books I read with things I want to go back and read. Sheri Dew's last book looks like it has a green wig sprouting out of the top. That's the sign of a good book. Some just have one lone strand of hot pink Post-It-Notery hanging out the top.

I also really appreciate nail clippers. Is it not the coolest thing? Who in the world thought of sticking two pieces of metal together like that? Very clever. And they're so handy! They're great for clipping off price tags, stray threads, nails, you name it! I'm so thankful I live in the modern day with these handy gadgets.

I'm so very thankful for my microwave oven. I pray often prayers of gratitude for my microwave. It is just amazing how fast I can whip out a meal. And it gives us so much extra time to do wonderful things.

And aren't we grateful for those baby carrots? Hours saved on peeling and cutting. And sunscreen is huge. Absolutely miraculous. And who can say enough thanks for those mapping programs on the Internet. I have literally saved hours and hours of recreational driving (that's what I call it when I'm lost).

We appreciate answering machines, moisture lotion, those groovy toggles on bracelets so we can put them on alone, and control top pantyhose. We're thankful for cell phones (although sometimes they're annoying) and high-lighter markers.

I'm grateful for LDS.org. Man, I thought the Topical Guide was hot stuff. Now I've got the whole enchilada right at my fingertips. I can hear conference talks over and over. I can look up all the talks and articles I want. I can study my scriptures in ways I never could before. I can keep up on worldwide news of the Church. It's totally awesome. So to all the dear folk who work on that, thanks so much!

A woman recently asked me how Mormons stay so happy. This is how I do. Every day, all day long, I am grateful. I'm grateful that my legs work and I can stand in the shower (my friend can't). I'm grateful for my pillow and my blanket and include those in my prayer most nights (my friends in Africa don't have these). I'm so very thankful for e-mail. I'm thankful for toilet paper, and air conditioning, and my son's sunny smile, and curling irons. All day long it goes. And I'm so very happy!

So my days unfold—full of little prayers, thanking Heavenly Father for all the little things that make my life easier. To all of you in the world who have responded to inspiration and creativity, thank you. Thank you for blessing my life. I appreciate it.

SPIRITUAL VALLEYS

Carolyn J. Rasmus

President Brigham Young once made a statement that has impressed me very much. In a quiet moment with his secretary and two others, someone asked, "President Young, why is it that the Lord is not always at our side promoting universal happiness and seeing to it that the needs of people are met, caring especially for His Saints? Why is it so difficult at times?"

President Young answered, "Because man is destined to be a God, and he must be able to demonstrate that he is for God and to develop his own resources so that he can act independently and yet humbly." Then he added, "It is the way it is because we must learn to be righteous in the dark" (Brigham Young's Office Journal, 28 January 1857).

For me, learning to be "righteous in the dark" is part of my challenge in life. I have found times of spiritual abundance alternating with feelings of perceived abandonment. In pondering this idea one day, I wrote the following in my personal journal: "Because of my experiences prior to joining the

Church I expected that following my baptism I would experience one big spiritual high. The past ten years have taught me otherwise. Instead, I find that mountain-top experiences are separated by valleys, even deserts. I struggle with ambiguities and contradictions. I am disturbed by discrepancies between gospel principles and practices. Often I have more questions than answers, and, like Nephi, I often feel encompassed about because of the temptations and sins which do so easily beset me.

"However, after passing through spiritual deserts where I have struggled with problems, I gain new insights and understandings and realize how finite my own vision is. I no longer equate ease and comfort with happiness and contentment, but am in the process of coming to better understand the peace and joy spoken of in the gospel. No wonder our Heavenly Father, whose knowledge is perfect, provides us with spiritual valleys as well as spiritual peaks."

LISTENING

Hilary Weeks

I love aspen trees. Not so much for the way they look or for their brilliant yellow autumn leaves. I like the sound they make. The breeze makes the leaves and twigs "click" together, creating a calming, mesmerizing melody. It is unique to aspen trees. I haven't noticed it when I am around other trees. In our yard, we have only a couple of aspens, so I have to stand close to them if I want to hear the soothing tap. Standing in a grove of aspens I can hear much better.

But I have recently had to evaluate my listening skills. My 11-year-old daughter was frustrated with me one day after school. She told me I don't listen very well. She said that there have been times when she is telling me something when I will take a phone call or talk to one of the other kids. She was absolutely right.

Just a few months before this conversation, she needed me to pull her loose tooth. I took a small piece of tissue and pinched the tooth. I tugged and tugged, but it wouldn't come—the tooth needed a little more time. Before long, she was back, asking for me to try again because the tooth was bothering her so much. I was committed to pulling that tooth. I tried three times, and finally, it popped out, but I really had to get under that tooth! She went to the bathroom to rinse her mouth and I heard her yell, "Mom! You pulled the wrong tooth!" I told her I knew she was joking around. She replied, "No, you really pulled the wrong tooth!" I looked. Sure enough, I saw the tooth I was supposed to pull, dangling by a thread. I pulled it, too, as I heard my husband say from the other room, "Please tell me that was a baby tooth."

I had definitely not been listening.

We have laughed about that since then and I have been better about listening. I don't want her to feel unimportant because I am not listening. When she wants to talk, even if it is not at a convenient time, I listen.

I have also tried to listen to someone else in my life—the Holy Ghost. It is true what they say—His voice is soft, subtle, quiet, and whisper-like. I have learned to seek His voice, learn what it sounds like to me, and trust that I am really hearing Him. I especially enjoy the quiet messages, counsel, and guidance that enter my mind after I pray and then listen. I stay on my knees and listen. I wouldn't want Him to feel like I don't care what He has to say.

It's like listening to the aspen trees—the more there are,

the better I can hear their sound. The more I seek the Spirit and strive to be worthy of His companionship, the more I feel Him there. He has brought me strength and answers. He has put thoughts into my mind so I understand situations more fully. He has become my companion.

The Holy Ghost really is and does all that Parley P. Pratt testified when he said:

The Spirit "quickens all the intellectual faculties, increases, enlarges, expands, and purifies all the natural passions and affections, and adapts them, by the gift of wisdom, to their lawful use. It inspires, develops, cultivates, and matures all the fine-toned sympathies, joys, tastes, kindred feelings, and affections of our nature. It inspires virtue, kindness, goodness, tenderness, gentleness, and charity. It develops beauty of person, form, and features. It tends to health, vigor, animation, and social feeling. It invigorates all the faculties of the physical and intellectual man. It strengthens and gives tone to the nerves. In short, it is, as it were, marrow to the bone, joy to the heart, light to the eyes, music to the ears, and life to the whole being" (*Key to the Science of Theology* [Salt Lake City: Deseret Book Company, 1978], 61).

YOU ARE HERE

Kim A. Nelson

When I was a young, married man, my wife and I lived on the Navajo reservation. One day, a friend—a very old Navajo medicine man—asked me a favor. Although he had traveled extensively as a young man, he had not been too far from the reservation in many years. He told me he had heard of a new shopping mall in Albuquerque, New Mexico, and he wanted to see what it looked like.

As I recall, the mall was said to have a huge indoor fountain, and that intrigued him. The idea of an indoor stream was just too much for him to resist, although the mall was several hundred miles away. He said he was not sure his truck would make the trip and that he did not want to leave the reservation without reliable transportation. He thought my car had a better chance of successfully making the roundtrip. (I remember thinking that was not so much an endorsement of my car as a confession of how really unreliable his truck was.) Looking back, I think that perhaps after a long winter he had a bit of cabin fever and wanted to share the trip with me.

Our all-day adventure is one I remember with real fondness. We passed the time that day talking about the world in general and solving all kinds of problems, as friends do when they take the time to talk. He reminisced about his boyhood, how he was taken to the all-Indian boarding school to receive his education. He said that at first he hated the school but had over time come to appreciate the experience. It was there he learned to read, and that gift had been one he had taken advantage of throughout his life. He was a voracious reader and loved to talk about current events and history. He recalled being taught by his father and grandfather in the traditional ways of the Navajo. He told me about his time in the army during World War I. It was a great ride, and I enjoyed listening to his wisdom and insights.

We got to the mall and spent the bulk of the day in and around the city. We shopped, had lunch and dinner, and just generally enjoyed a wonderful time. The trip back was uneventful, and we arrived home safely. Just before turning onto the road to his hogan, I asked what part of the trip was his favorite. I don't know what I expected to hear, but his answer was a real surprise.

"That is easy," he said. "I liked the 'you are here' sign at the mall." He described how much he had appreciated the mall map and directory with the red pointing finger labeled "You are here."

"It is wonderful to know where you are," he said. "Once I knew that, I could go anywhere on that map and return safely. I was not lost."

This little parable has remained with me every day since that time. Wouldn't it be nice to know, every day and absolutely, where we are?

I have tried over the years to recognize the "you are here" signs in my life. The global positioning apparatus of prayer, obedience, scripture study, and the promptings of the Holy Ghost allow me to locate my position daily. Knowing our Father and recognizing His loving invitation to me to rejoin Him keeps my destination in focus.

I know if I can keep track of where I am, I can find my way home.

THE SUNDAY SACRIFICE

Emily Watts

This past summer, our ward building was closed for a couple of months for "Asbestos Abatement." Isn't that a fancy way of saying they needed to clean up a mess from materials used years ago when the chapel was constructed? I love saying it—it's so lyrical—Asbestos Abatement, Asbestos Abatement . . .

Anyway, such a project poses no great hardship in my neighborhood in Utah, where we have a lot of apartments and are so densely populated that there are two more LDS meetinghouses within three blocks of ours. The three wards that normally met in our building were parceled out to those other two locations. No problem. Until we heard that our ward had drawn the time slot of 3:00 to 6:00 P.M. for our block of Sunday meetings.

Ugh! I think it would be safe to say that nobody was looking forward to this. We had been meeting from 9:00 to 12:00, and people were not thrilled about having to wait all day long just to get into church, not to mention getting home so late afterward. We muttered and groused for a while but soon recognized that we were being ridiculously whiny about this. There really was not another option, so eventually everyone settled into the idea and agreed to make the "big sacrifice."

I don't know how it was for others, but a really interesting thing happened to me during those two months. It turned out that I was much more focused on the Sabbath day when I spent most of the day anticipating the worship service. I realized how apt I had been on the earlier schedule to come home after church, kick off my shoes, and relax into more temporal pursuits. Now I had hours to read, to put the finishing touches on a lesson, to sit down with the whole family for a nice meal, and then to cap it all off with partaking of the sacrament and enjoying my church meetings. It was really quite wonderful!

We're back in our own building now, the asbestos having been successfully abated, but I'm trying to keep putting into practice the principles I learned in those two months. I'm trying not to stamp the Sabbath "done" when the three-hour block I spend in church is over. And guess what—just as the scriptures promise, when I truly make Sunday the Lord's day, I'm a happier, better person!

MIRACLES

Merrilee Boyack

A miracle happened this morning. Did you see it? The sun rose—all by itself. It was beautiful—pink and then a brilliant yellow and then pure white. A miracle.

A few weeks ago I sat down for lunch in a cafeteria at BYU-Idaho Education Week next to a young man who was sitting all alone. He was a handsome young man in his early 20s, and I'm sure he didn't expect a middle-aged (chronologically speaking) woman to sit down next to him. I found out his name is Justin. And he was an interesting young man. He had fallen into inactivity from the Church at age ten and was now in the process of coming back. He spoke of how he had studied the gospel and many other religions for four hours a day. He had led an interesting life, said he was on his 35th job.

"It makes sense," he said, referring to the Church. "It makes more sense than any other religion."

"That's because it's true," I said. He smiled.

"But I have a hard time just . . . accepting the whole thing," he replied.

"Ah, so your problem is faith." I smiled back.

"Yup, that's it. I have trouble with that whole faith-thing." I sat back and listened.

"I guess I want to see a miracle," he said.

"So you want a sign to prove it to you?" I asked.

"Well, not exactly. I just want to see a miracle," he answered.

"Well, you're looking at one," I said. He looked at me quizzically.

And I told him my story:

When I was a baby, I was born severely cross-eyed. My parents realized that I didn't notice things—didn't smile, didn't reach for toys, etc. They took me to the finest eye doctor in the world who was at the University of Michigan at the time. I grew up in Detroit, Michigan.

The doctor examined me carefully and came back to my parents. "I am sorry, but there is nothing that can be done. Your daughter will go blind and will have to be institutionalized for the rest of her life. Just go home and enjoy what time you have with her."

Can you imagine how devastating this news was to my parents? The entire family, my parents and my three older sisters, grieved and prayed. A short time later, Elder Harold B.

Lee came to town for stake conference. He was a member of the Quorum of the Twelve Apostles at the time. My parents made an appointment with him and brought me, their six-month-old daughter, to him. They begged him to give me a blessing, which he did.

Elder Lee blessed me that my eyes would never stand in the way of anything I wanted to do in this life and promised that I would be compensated for any loss.

My faithful parents then took me back to the eye doctor. "I know this news is difficult to accept," he said, "but there is nothing I can do." "Please," they begged him, "please just examine her one more time." Probably out of a desire to have my parents leave him alone, the doctor agreed.

After a long time he came back. "I don't know what has happened, but it's a miracle. We can operate."

My parents knew that a miracle had occurred. And after six surgeries, I could see normally. It truly was a miracle.

The years have passed and after school, law school, and reading nonstop for over forty years, and after more surgery (LASIK), I am walking around without glasses. All evidences of unbelievable miracles.

"So there you have it," I said, "I'm a miracle!"

Justin was pleased. "Well, I guess I've seen a miracle," he conceded.

"Yes, you have," I affirmed. "But frankly, the whole thing is a miracle, Justin. Just look around you." He smiled.

"It's true," I said again. "The gospel is true. That's the best miracle." And we parted ways.

Oh, Justin, can't you see the miracles all around you? The new baby that is born. The ocean waves. Your hands. The love of our families. The unfolding of a rose. Miracles all. Big and small. Do we need miracles to have faith? No. But our faith is strengthened by all the miracles we see.

Jacob describes it well in the Book of Mormon, "Behold, my soul delighteth in proving unto my people the truth of the coming of Christ; . . . and all things which have been given of God from the beginning of the world, unto man, are the typifying of him" (2 Nephi 11:4).

All things testify of Christ. All the miracles, big and small, tell us that He lives! That He loves us! And that He has created this world for us.

And the most amazing miracle of all to me is that I know that Heavenly Father knows me. Out of all the billions of his children, He knows me. He loves ME. THAT is a miracle. He knows you, too, Justin. I hope you know that.

THE REAL YOU

Hilary Weeks

My friend Heather smiles all the time. I know because she is in my ward and I watch her. She smiles at the person giving the talk, the family singing the musical number, the Sunday School teacher. She lives in the house behind me, and when I see her in the neighborhood . . . she's smiling. When I pass her on the road she smiles and waves!

I have known a few people like Heather, who smile a lot. I want to be more like them.

Sometimes when I'm doing the dishes or sweeping the floor, my seven-year-old daughter will say to me, "What's wrong?"

I answer, "Nothing, why?"

"Because your face looks like you're mad."

Oops. I've heard it takes more facial muscles to frown than to smile. So I figure if it is less work, I may as well smile more. I practice smiling in the store. I smile in the car. Even when no one is around, I practice smiling. At first it didn't feel very natural, and when I looked at my smile in the mirror it looked more like a smirk. But I think my muscles are getting stronger because recently I smiled in the mirror and it looked quite pleasant.

There are a lot of things like smiling that I want to improve about myself. I imagine we all feel that way. I have a little philosophy about becoming and being the "real you" or in other words, the person you want and know you can be.

To some extent we know our strengths and weaknesses. Often we notice someone else's strength and wish we were more that way—like Heather, for instance. My philosophy is the good quality we notice in someone else is a quality we actually already possess but have not yet developed. It is in us, we just need to watch and learn from another's example. The fact we notice the strength in someone else is our inner spirit's desire to develop that quality.

Here's another example. We used to live in Colorado. I had a friend named Linda. Anytime I asked Linda for help she said yes in the most sincere and truly willing way. I never felt as though I was putting her out—she seemed so genuinely happy to help. I wanted to be more like Linda, and while that skill has definitely not come easily to me, I have improved. Just recently I offered help to a friend and she complimented my willingness and sincere desire to help! That was one of the best compliments I have ever received, and it made me want to keep trying.

Who is the real you? Do you want to smile more? Do you want to be organized? Do you want to be a person who loves and accepts everyone? Do you want to have a home in which everyone knows they are welcome? Do you want to make the world's best cheese ball? (That is one of my strengths. Let me know and I can totally help you out.)

It is pretty easy to figure out. Just think of someone's example that you admire. Watch as they use that quality. You could even ask them how they do it—get a little one-on-one advice!

It is a pattern with which we are already familiar. We know how to look to the Savior for our ultimate example. And along the road of life, His qualities can be found in those around us. Following those examples can help us become our very best. Our weaknesses truly can become our strengths and our strengths can be a blessing to others. It is part of the cycle of becoming the "real you."

And just in case you were wondering, yes, I am practicing smiling right now.

Today and every day, I want to be SOMEBODY.

HELP! I'M SURROUNDED!

Chris Stewart

Not long ago, as I was kneeling in prayer, I began to suddenly feel very humble and even a little scared. I was starting to realize how much my family and I were reliant on God. I thought of how I worry for my children: my son on his mission, my other sons at college, and my younger kids who are having to grow up in such an evil world. I thought about how I worry about my business. I realize how fragile it is and that although we have been successful, there is always the feeling that the whole thing could come crashing down. I thought about how I worry about staying healthy, getting all my writing done, writing anything that is good!

As I thought, I realized again and again that I needed God in all things, and that nothing was assured.

Later that day I read in Helaman 4 about how the Nephites were always so outnumbered by the Lamanites. The Lamanites had spent the previous 600 years trying to destroy them and so the Nephites were constantly surrounded and always felt vulnerable to attack. The Nephite's peace, like mine, was also very fragile.

In verse 25, after the Nephites had become wicked and prideful and had forgotten the Lord, it says, "Therefore the Lord did cease to preserve them by his miraculous and matchless power."

I realized that we are all in the same boat as the Nephites. We are often outnumbered in life and feel surrounded by worries and problems. There are always things that can go wrong, but it is by miracles that we are sustained and not overcome by events of these times in which we live.

Yet, like the ancient people of God, if we remember the Lord, he will always sustain us by his "miraculous and matchless power." The question isn't *can* God sustain us, or *will* He sustain us, it is only a question of whether we are humble enough that we *let* Him sustain us.

The miraculous sustaining is always there. It is up to us if we will accept it.

ORANGE EYE SHADOW VS. AMAZING GRACE

Cherie Call

I like makeup. In that sense, I'm really a girly girl. When I go to the mall I love how the eye shadow colors look all lined up next to each other on the counters, and even though I know I'll never wear super sparkly florescent orange, for some reason I'm just glad it's there at the MAC counter, just brightening up the world in its own special way.

I know everyone has a different philosophy about makeup. Some people don't need it, some people don't want it, some people think it's evil, and I respect that. But I just never feel fully dressed until I have makeup on. And sometimes I think it's just fun.

My six-month-old baby girl, Sydney, loves watching everything I do. One of the things she really loves is when I have her strapped onto me in one of those soft baby carrier front pack things while I get ready in the morning. I originally tried this once so she'd stop crying, but now it's something she likes a lot. She loves all the little brushes, and she looks at her little eyes in all the tiny mirrors inside the blush and eye shadow compacts. We smile at each other, and I try to see if she looks like me.

Many times I look in the big mirror at both of us, and after I smear some skin-colored liquid on my face that's supposed to even out the pink blotches and hide a few lines, I notice how absolutely, insanely perfect Sydney's face is. She has heavenly, soft, smooth skin, naturally rosy cheeks and lips, and sparkly blue eyes. It would be a sick joke to put any of this wannabe pretty stuff on her truly beautiful face. I realize that no matter how much I pay, no matter how much time I spend on it, or how many worldly remedies I try, my face will never in a million years look like hers does right now. Time and tears and even smiles have made these lines and imperfections in my skin. There's no turning back.

And then it blows my mind to realize that Jesus is actually capable of making me just that new and beautiful and innocent on the inside, just like Sydney, every time I repent. I can be baby perfect every morning when I wake up and start fresh and ask for His grace and let Him carry my burdens. It's an amazing miracle!

I say a silent prayer in my heart that Sydney will know all about Jesus and that she'll have a long, beautiful life full of smiles and even a few tears, even if that does mean she'll get some serious lines. It's worth it.

Then I say another little prayer that she'll never wear super sparkly florescent orange eye shadow. Unless it looks awesome on her. But not till she's like twenty years old. That's a topic for another day.

TOMORROW'S ASSIGNMENT

Merrilee Boyack

My poor mother had four daughters and then a son. My sisters and I have spent the last forty-plus years analyzing everything my mother ever said and did. We have dissected and discussed her behavior, her parenting, her appearance, you name it. My poor mother. She didn't stand a chance.

I, on the other hand, was blessed with four sons. A couple of years ago, I asked my oldest son, Connor, who was then twenty-two, "Son, how do you feel I did as a mother?" He looked at me and said, "Huh?" I repeated my question, "You know, how do you feel I did as a mom in raising you?"

"Fine."

"Do you think I did a good job or did I do a lot of damage or what?"

"I said fine."

I persisted, "Well I'm sorry if I messed up or made a lot of mistakes or whatever." He replied, "No sweat."

So at a later date, I asked his next-oldest brother, "Brennan, how do you feel I did as a mom?"

"OK, I guess."

"Well, I'm sorry for all the mistakes I made in raising you. I know that I could have done better and I hope you can forgive me."

"Sure."

Not to be outdone, I asked their younger brothers who each replied in similar fashion. Actually, one son was tremendously eloquent, "Real good, Mom." He's my favorite. Can't remember which one it was but he's my favorite.

You see, guys don't analyze the whole mothering thing that much. Can I tell you how blessed I am? Not only do they not pound to death everything I ever said or did as a mom, they don't remember it! What a gift I have been given! And I certainly appreciate it.

For those of you who were not so lucky and have reproduced hyper-analytical types like my mother did, take heart.

Think what it must have been like to be a mother in Israel, following Moses around and having your kids say for FORTY YEARS, "Are we there yet? Are we there yet? Are we there yet?" What was it like for Sarah and Lehi, where their family home evenings ended up with two brothers tying up their younger brother and trying to kill him? Now, we've had that happen, but they always untied him by the end of the evening.

What was it like to be the mother of young Alma? "I told you time and again, do NOT play with those Mosiah boys ever again!" and then sitting there crying at their missionary farewell saying, "Who knew?"

Being a mother can be a scary adventure. I think the Lord doesn't give us any background on these kids for a reason. Talk about a leap of faith!

But you know what, He asks one thing of us as moms . . . "Will you wake up again tomorrow and love them?" Frankly, He asks the same thing of all of us—aunts, wives, sisters, teachers, moms, friends, grandmas—"Will you wake up again tomorrow and love some more?"

To which, I wax eloquent—"OK."

LAUNDRY ON MY BIRTHDAY?!

Daryl Hoole

You're doing the washing on your birthday?" I was appalled. My mother was going to spend her birthday doing the family laundry. Such a thing was unthinkable to my five-year-old mind. Vowing to my young self that I would never ever in all my life do the laundry on my birthday, I felt keenly disappointed in my mother for not planning her life better. A birthday is HUGE when you're five, and I couldn't imagine anything important enough to interfere with the day.

For my mother, the washing was an all-day labor—filling the Dexter washing machine's double tubs with water, stirring up a pan of starch on one burner of the stove, warming a pan of bluing (to make the white clothing even whiter) on another, feeding each item of clothing through the wringer from the wash tub to the rinse tubs, then passing everything back through the wringer to the clothes basket and finally hanging the wash on the line to dry—and to me, it was the most un-birthday-like thing anyone could possibly do. It was years before I realized that maybe my mother *wanted* to do the laundry that day, even though it was her birthday. Maybe my mother wanted to have clean clothing for her family even more than she wanted personal pleasures.

Well, lots of birthdays have come and gone for me, and it has become clear that life is not really about how much fun we can have on our birthdays. It's not even about whether we were the generation who used the double tub Dexter; or the previous one who hauled water from the spring, heated it over an open fire, and made their own soap; or the current one who just sets a dial and presses the "on" button. Life is about doing our duty, whatever it may be. It's about serving those we love.

If you've been experiencing a "wintry" mood lately because your workload is heavy, life seems dull and dreary, you're tired of the routine, your motivation is at a low ebb, or your priorities need a realignment, perhaps a fresh perspective may help. Following are three suggestions for a spring tune-up:

FOCUS ON THE BIG PICTURE. Considering the eternal perspective can make a world of difference—you're not just keeping house. Rather, you're making a home—one that can last forever.

LET YOURSELF FEEL "DONE." There is always another towel that someone just tossed in the hamper. So, the smart thing to do is say to yourself, "I've done the laundry for today. That towel is for tomorrow's wash," and move on, feeling "done."

FIGHT BOREDOM. Boredom sets in when we're no longer excited about what we're doing. When this is the case, it's time to try a new idea, develop a new talent, be of service somewhere, or engage in a new project. We're bored when we concentrate on the process, rather than on the results.

I've long since forgiven my mother for doing the wash on her birthday. Instead I revere her for always doing her duty cheerfully and taking care of our family to the very best of her ability. She would smile and shake her head at our discussions about the seeming futility, the endlessness, and the boredom of housework and say, "Ladies, it's time for a spring tune-up."

SIGNS OF FAITH

Pamela H. Hansen

At a recent Time Out for Women event, I sat listening to one of the speakers while watching the American Sign Language interpreter. I admired the graceful way she moved her hands into various gestures that enabled those who couldn't hear the words to experience them. There was a beautiful spirit that radiated from the two women who took turns sharing their gift of translation. In addition to the signing they did with their hands, their faces were full of animation as they mouthed the words that were spoken. I was impressed at their multi-tasking skills of listening and "talking" at the same time—something my children desperately wish I could master.

What brought me to tears was when Hilary Weeks got up to sing. As her angelic melodies filled the room, these women took turns interpreting. However, during the sing-along, I watched as the women participating in the sign-language group were singing along, using their hands. It humbled me to see them singing about joy and about the Savior. They appeared to be much more actively singing than what I have witnessed in some church meetings. These women were enthusiastically paying tribute to their Father in Heaven; although their voices were silent, their praises rang out loud and clear. It was quite awe-inspiring to witness.

The Bible Dictionary, under the topic of "Faith," states that "Faith is a principle of action and of power . . . true faith always moves its possessor to some kind of physical and mental action; it carries an assurance of the fulfillment of the things hoped for."

How much more actively can we demonstrate our faith? Joseph Smith did not simply pray that the plates would be protected in his care; he actively took every precaution to assure that they did not fall into the hands of those with malicious intent. He creatively came up with ways, under the direction of Heavenly Father, to guarantee the plates would be preserved to fill their purpose while under his watch.

I think of those talented American Sign Language translators as I consider how I can more clearly demonstrate my faith through my actions. I think of them as I sing. It helps me to sing with a little more heartfelt conviction, which seems to fill my heart with even more praise of Him who gave us the gift of music.

THE BREAD OF LIFE

Sharon G. Larsen

like to bake rolls. It is amazing to me to mix up yeast and flour, milk and eggs, and watch the magic happen. The yeast slowly, almost imperceptibly, expands through the mixture, causing it to quietly move and rise. After I have added all of the ingredients and mixed it together well, I cover it with a clean dishtowel and forget it. A few hours later I remember, "Oh yes, I have roll dough in a bowl on the cupboard, waiting for my attention." If I don't get back to the dough in time, it will raise up over the edge of the bowl, spread down the side of the bowl and onto the cupboard.

Then the "therapy" begins. I can punch it and poke it, mash it and spread it out, or squash it together and it just keeps coming back and rising again. That is a desirable characteristic when the yeast is good yeast.

The Lord condemned "bad yeast," or bad leaven, as He called it (see Matthew 16:6, 11, 12). He cautioned His disciples to be careful of the leaven of the Sadducees and

Pharisees. These people were anti-Christ's who taught the philosophies of men mixed with some scripture. They were the voices of the "world" at the time. They were articulate, smart, maybe even glamorous, charismatic, and clothed in costly apparel. They were powerful people with influence. Today we would call them "opinion-makers." People listened to them to learn what they "should" be thinking about, what "cool" people were talking about, what problems existed that they hadn't even thought about, maybe even what problems they had in their own lives they didn't realize they had.

This kind of evil "leaven" infiltrates, moves, spreads, and rises, almost without us noticing what is happening. And before we know it, it has spread far beyond any boundaries. No matter how often it is discredited or criticized, it just keeps coming back and has continued to rise and contaminate civilization for the past 2,000 years.

I became aware of the difference between good leaven and bad leaven in a sacrament meeting with my three-year-old grandson Jake. His mother had brought treats to pacify her boys during church. When the tray of sacramental bread was being passed down our row, Jake whispered in my ear, "Tell them we don't need that bread, we brought our own treats."

A three-year-old could not understand the symbolism and sacredness of the broken bread. M&Ms seemed a lot more enticing! But that incident made me ask myself *Do I prefer my own treats or "mess of pottage" over the Bread of Life the Lord so freely offers to me? Do I give more time and attention listening to or watching or reading what the "Sadducees and Pharisees" of the world are saying, than I do what prophets, seers, and revelators are telling me?*

If I would "purge out . . . the old leaven" (1 Corinthians 5:6–7) of the world and partake of the good leaven, the Bread of Life, I could help the kingdom of God expand and bubble and spread throughout the world, or at least, my world.

A MUST SEE!
BEAUTIFUL INSIDE!

Cherie Call

When I got married a few years ago, I moved into the house that my husband had already owned for a year or two. He had previously lived in the house with three other guys. So when I moved in, I painted some walls, put up some curtains, and we both changed a lot of things about the house to make it more like a home. It's been a good place to live, and we've really enjoyed our neighborhood and our friends here, but we recently decided it was time to start fresh and build a new home we could move into together. It's been an exciting process and also a big learning experience.

The home building company we've been using has a big warehouse full of all the different counters, cabinets, carpets, doors, etc. from which you can choose for your home. There were so many decisions to be made that it took us a few days to get through it all. We spent so much time at it that I would dream about it at night. In my dreams, my ten-month-old baby was smiling and running at top speed on the nice new carpet in the empty rooms. When I woke up, though, I was faced with a challenge, one that I still face now. We have to sell the house we already have.

For the past few weeks, we've been scrubbing, painting, scraping, mowing, and much more, to beautify our house. I've had a lot of time to look at the details in our current house that I had not thought very much about before. Mostly, I'm discovering imperfections right before my eyes that I had not previously seen. Sometimes this has been really overwhelming and depressing. We have a little TV in the kitchen, and I sometimes watch the cooking programs or the extreme makeover girly kinds of shows while I do the dishes. The worst anxiety happens when I'm flipping through the channels and come across one of those home-selling shows on HGTV. I panic and think to myself, "but we don't have the time or money to gut the whole house and build a fireplace! All I've done is dust!!"

We have done a lot of little things that have made a big difference. It's been amazing to see how brightly the sink fixtures shine once I scrape off the hard water buildup and then polish them. The more we've gotten done, the more excited I've been to move into our new house, but I've also noticed that our current house is a lot nicer place to live now. Anyone could come over at a moment's notice to look at it, so we take special care to make sure it looks great every day before we leave. Lately we've been coming home to a fresh, clean house. I know for most people this is totally normal, but for me it's kind of new, I hate to admit.

Why am I telling you all of this? It's kind of made me think about how my life is like all of this. I have this warehouse in my mind of how I want things to be. I want the perfect attitude. I want to lose a few pounds. I want to write amazing songs. I want to be a better person, do more, be more spiritual and intelligent, be a better wife, mother, friend, etc., etc., etc. If I think too much about it I get overwhelmed and don't do any of it. I seem to do my best when I first cut myself a little slack and love myself enough to feel comfortable in my own skin. Then I can do one little thing at a time to get ready for the "new" me. In the meantime, the old me is a pretty nice person to live with because I'm on the right track. Prayer and faith really help a lot. God is always anxious to tell you how great you are but then also to help you become even better.

I still get depressed when I watch HGTV, and I'm still stressed about selling our house, but I can laugh about it and know that I'm doing everything I can. I hope I can have the same attitude about the process of becoming the person I've always wanted to be.

THE TOW TRUCK PARABLE

Laurel Christensen

When I was in college, I took a summer road trip from Utah to California with a friend of the male persuasion. It was a fun trip. We did all the usual "Southern California" things for a couple of days and had a great time. But, on the return drive, my 1985 Chevy Cavalier decided it was done. All the fun had just worn the little car out. At the last call box between the California and Nevada desert portion of I-15, the car died. Neither of us had any idea what was wrong exactly, though I finally had to confess to my friend that my mechanic had warned me not to drive the car over 55 mph or else one of the belts might not make it—information that certainly would have been helpful prior to his taking his turn at the wheel.

It seemed to take a few hours for the tow truck to arrive. And when you're in the middle of a desert, nearly two hours from the nearest city (Las Vegas, NV), you just don't have a lot of choices. It is not the time to do a price comparison on available towing services. I remember the tow truck driver's name was Donny and that he said he could get us to Vegas for some obscene amount of money. But we had no choice. Donny told us to get in the cab of his truck while he hooked up my tired little car.

As my friend and I walked to the front of the very large tow truck, we opened the passenger side door to discover two bucket seats in the front and a bench seat in the back. The only problem was that the space between the frame of the door and the back of the front seat, even when the seat was folded forward, was not very big. It was either my 6'0" friend or my not-so-petite self who would have to get through that narrow triangular space—perhaps a 12" opening at its widest place. I looked at him. He looked at me. We knew there was only one option.

As I stepped up onto the step of the truck, my left foot somehow got awkwardly tangled in the seatbelt. At the same time, my right foot got tangled in the very long strap of my purse (worn across the shoulder as was the fashion of the time). There I was, precariously perched on the step of the truck with both feet tangled. I knew there was only one thing to do. I had to make a dive for that back bench . . . through the widest part of the opening. I still don't know how I got through there onto that seat, but I knew that it would be a while before I would be able to actually look at my friend again. Finally, as I was lying on my stomach with my embarrassed face buried in the seat, it hit me how the whole thing must have looked from his viewpoint, and I began to laugh.

When I was finally able to roll over and sit up, I noticed the backseat had a full-size window, with a handle that could be used to roll the window down. Immediately, I thought, *Well, that's dumb. Why would there be a full-size window for this backseat but not a door. . . .* I grabbed the door handle and opened the back door. I couldn't believe it. There had been a DOOR there the entire time. No one was supposed to fit through that triangular opening. The door provided the typical entrance to a backseat.

My friend swears he didn't see it either (though I'm still not convinced), but as I sat in that backseat, thinking of all the effort I put into getting in there, I couldn't help but think about my life. And, of course, the story means much more to me now after many more life experiences.

So often, I am intent on seeing something the way it appears to be. When I see a problem or a situation that I need to fix or get through, I'm not inclined to patiently seek a solution. Rather, I find the solution that seems to be the only option and then just go for it, often making things harder or longer (or more awkward) than things need to be. What if, during those times, instead of reacting quickly, I would just step back and look at what lies before me? I suspect I just might be able to see the more obvious, or better, path toward success. And better yet, what if I would step back and look and then involve the Lord? Surely HE knows and could help me see a better way, yes, even the best way.

"For my thoughts are not your thoughts, neither are your ways my ways, saith the Lord" (Isaiah 55:8).

A BAG OF CATS

Kim A. Nelson

A therapist friend recently shared a story with me that has caused me to reflect on the assumptions I make as I communicate with others. She was driving down a country road and saw a man throw a bag from his truck. She noticed the bag was moving and pulled over to see what was inside. As an animal lover, she was horrified to discover that the bag contained several kittens. The man was obviously trying to get rid of what he saw as a problem.

The cats were agitated and frightened. She was worried that being tossed from a moving vehicle might have injured them. In an effort to calm them and assess the damage, she opened the bag. What she discovered was that the cats were not aware of her benevolent motivation. Rather than being calmed by the sight of her face as she opened the bag, they became even more agitated. They did everything in their power to escape. They lashed out in an effort to defend themselves from what they perceived to be a continuation of the threat to their safety.

With some effort and a good deal of pain, she managed to keep them in the bag and take them to a veterinarian. After the cats were cared for and taken to a shelter, my friend took a moment to reflect upon her experience. She realized that the cats had no way of knowing her intention as she opened the bag. In fact, the best bet, based on their experience, was that the person who held the bag was most likely out to hurt them.

As she related the story to me the next day, it was easy for us to see a parallel between the cats in that bag and many of the people we had tried to help over the years. Unfortunately, many people have learned that the interactions they have with others can be painful. Their life's experiences have conditioned them to be cautious and suspicious. In many cases, they assume a threat and respond like the cats in the bag.

We all want to be safe. We don't want to be in pain. Sometimes, when I've been hurt or am tired, I'm sure to those who approach me I seem like a bag of desperate cats.

That's a lesson I need to remember as I interact with others. I need to make sure that I communicate in a way that reassures and makes my intentions plain. I need to do all I can to provide a pain-free place to talk. I need to remember not to assume, on those days when I feel as though I have been thrown out, that *everyone* is out do me harm.

Perhaps there might even be a good soul looking out for

me on the lonely road. There may be a friend or even a stranger who only wants to help me get the attention I need to heal my wounds. As I reflect on who my neighbor is and what kind of neighbor I want to be, it is no surprise that I am reminded of another neighbor and the road from Jerusalem to Jericho.

ARE WE BEING WISE?

Dean Hughes

Sit down for a sec.

Take a breath.

Have you forgotten already?

Remember that conference talk? The one by Elder M. Russell Ballard? He told us to be wise. He told us to cut out the "needless frills." Remember what you thought at the time? "He's right. I've got to stop overdoing."

We all made the same vow, didn't we? And now it's the season of peace and love, and what are we doing? Overdoing.

Here's what he said:

> "I would like to let you in on a little secret. Some of you have already learned it. If you haven't, it's time you knew. No matter what your family needs are or your responsibilities in the Church, there is no such a thing as "done." There will always be more we can do. There is always another family matter that needs attention,

another lesson to prepare, another interview to conduct, another meeting to attend. We just need to be wise in protecting our health and in following the counsel that President Hinckley has given often to just do the best that we can" ("O Be Wise," *Ensign*, Nov. 2006, 19).

Wow! He actually said that. An apostle. And we believed him.

But now Christmas is coming and you're getting yourself stressed, aren't you?

One of my pet peeves is hearing everyone ask, "So, are you ready for Christmas yet?" The question makes Christmas sound like this enormous project—something to get "done." Is that wise? Couldn't we fuss a little less this year and enjoy Christmas more? Couldn't we stop long enough, at least a time or two, to think what the season means?

When I was a little boy, my mom used to say, "They put up the Christmas decorations earlier every year." I've heard people say pretty much the same thing my whole life. Let's see, I'm over sixty now, so if "they" had actually moved up the Christmas hype every year, the decorations in the stores would all be up in July.

When we claim that "they" are "commercializing"

Christmas, aren't we really discovering something in ourselves and then looking for someone else to blame?

I love Christmas shopping. I like decorations. I like dinners and parties and family gatherings—and all the rest. And I like the food—way too much. But we all must like that stuff or we wouldn't make it happen again every year.

Still, somewhere in the middle of it all, let's take a breath. Let's hold the ones we love in our arms, maybe sit by the fire a few minutes. If we bake a little less, decorate a little less, skip a party or two, wouldn't it be worth it?

Elder Ballard also said that some people:

> . . . start believing that the programs they administer are more important than the people they serve. They complicate their service with needless frills and embellishments that occupy too much time, cost too much money, and sap too much energy (Ibid., 18).

He was talking about the way we do our Church work, but could the same words describe the way we do Christmas?

Sit down for a minute. Relax. Play some Christmas music.

Ask yourself whether there aren't some "embellishments" that could be dropped.

Do we blame the stores and the advertising because we don't want to admit what's actually missing from Christmas?

And don't we all know what that is?

I'm going to find some quiet time to listen to Handel's *Messiah* this year.

And I promise myself: I'm going to think more of Christ. My wife and I visited the Holy Land this last year. I can still see those Galilean hills in my mind. I'm going to think about that—the way I felt when I walked where He once walked.

We all know what's missing. It's Christ we want to invite to our celebration.

And we can't do it when we spend our whole time running.

So sit down for a sec.

Take a breath.

It's the nicest time of the year.

"GIGGLE BALL"

Camille Fronk Olson

ast Saturday we met again on the courts for some "fine" doubles play. Carol, Linda, Janice, and I have been getting together for nearly fifteen years—and a tennis court has become our most likely rendezvous spot.

Our brand of tennis is laughable to serious athletes, but we aren't playing for any outward acclaim. Our "matches" are a way to catch up on a few highlights in each others' lives, get some exercise, and receive an appreciated pat on the back. Linda calls it "giggle ball." Carol typically schedules the match and brings a basket holding about 50 semi-dead tennis balls that we volley back and forth over the net until the basket is empty. Then we fill it up again and go for a second round. The used balls slow down the pace and give us a feeling that we are still quite agile. No score is tracked, but nearly every shot receives enthusiastic praise, such as "Great hit!" "Perfect shot!" or "Nice volley!" Janice even has a song for some of the truly errant hits.

An hour passes quickly and soon we are gathering up the

balls for the last time. In these final minutes, news is shared—of a promotion at work, continued responsibilities in the Church, or the health of loved ones. In parting, Carol also shares a new vocabulary word and uses it in context—all in a way that reminds us of our friendship and gives us the benefit of the doubt on our intellects.

Our next rendezvous may be in two weeks or six months, but we are already looking forward to it. We all have heavy demands on our time and productivity, and although our cities of residence and circumstances in life differ, we continue to find time to play together. As I returned home Saturday from the latest of these gatherings, I wondered why. For starters, I came home feeling capable, invigorated, and loved. I took off for an hour of play even when my work at home and the office wasn't finished—and I was given renewed inspiration and energy to complete my tasks.

Can we ever have too many of such moments? Consider these "rules" for "giggle ball":

1. No one loses; everyone wins
2. We aren't competing against each other; no one keeps score
3. The talk is primarily praise-filled "one-liners"
4. Each person is an active participant
5. Only one person can hit the ball at a time, providing three potential cheerleaders for every return

6. We're a team where every person is needed

Are there ways to incorporate the giggle ball rules in family settings? In Church responsibilities? In the neighborhood? At the office? Look for an opportunity today to be a team player, where everyone is a winner.

GOING ONCE! GOING TWICE! SOLD!

Pamela H. Hansen

Not long ago, I attended my first art auction, purely out of curiosity. Strolling by many thousands of dollars worth of paintings to go on the auction block, I took a seat near the back.

As I waited for my sister to join me, I was quite fascinated by all I saw and heard. Several beautiful pieces—some more unusual than others—went on display. I watched various art enthusiasts bid on items by raising their hands as the auctioneer cried, "I've got $4,000 right down here," pointing to someone in the front, "who'll give me 5?" With some paintings, the bids climbed to large figures at an amazingly rapid pace. Others crept up slowly until the auctioneer finally announced, "Going once! Going twice! SOLD!"

One particularly odd work of art was set on display. The bidding began ". . . five hundred, six hundred, eight, nine hundred, one thousand . . ." it continued to climb. I noticed my sister arrive through the door to the gallery, which happened to be located just behind the auctioneer. She stood there for a moment, looking for me. Without thinking, I raised my hand and motioned to her.

You guessed it—she wasn't the only one who noticed my hand in the air. Quickly the auctioneer acknowledged my $2,000 bid.

I looked around in disbelief. Wait! That was not my intention! I frantically searched the rest of the spectators for anyone to outbid me.

The trained auctioneer, assuming his audience knew better, recognized my raised hand as a legitimate bid for the artwork. It didn't take a whole lot of time to realize I had certainly misjudged the proper time to wave during an auction!

We often judge the actions of others without knowing their true intent. What we perceive may be obvious to us, and yet, it may be quite (innocently!) unintentional. Then we act—or react—based on our understanding, which may well be a misunderstanding.

Moroni quotes his father, Mormon, who wisely taught, "And now, my brethren, seeing that ye know the light by which ye may judge, which light is the light of Christ, see that ye do not judge wrongfully; for with that same judgment which ye judge ye shall also be judged" (Moroni 7:18).

We may not always understand what others are experiencing. That is why we ought to "be swift to hear, slow to speak, slow to wrath" (James 1:19). We can also treat others with more kindness. I loved President Gordon B. Hinckley's comments in general conference last April. He stated, "There is no end to the good we can do, to the influence we can have with others. Let us not dwell on the critical or the negative. Let us pray for strength; let us pray for capacity and desire to assist others. Let us radiate the light of the gospel at all times and all places, that the Spirit of the Redeemer may radiate from us" ("The Need for Greater Kindness," *Ensign*, May 2006, 61).

As you can imagine, I was quickly praying for someone to love the painting more than I apparently did and set the bid higher. Whew! Was I ever relieved to see another woman raise her hand. I almost came home with a very interesting and expensive piece of artwork! As it was, I simply had to control my impulse to jump out of my seat and give her an enormous $2,000 hug!

SPRING SNOW

Emily Watts

It is mid-April. Yesterday, it was 70 degrees outside. Today, it snowed and snowed and snowed. I was so distressed! I looked out the window at all the beautiful flowers and blossoming trees in the blizzard and thought how sad it was that they were all going to freeze.

Late this afternoon, I walked down to the window to check on things. The snow had stopped. The sun wasn't out yet, but the roads were clear. The sidewalks were a little damp, but there was no sign whatsoever of the earlier snow. Most important, the flowers and trees were as vibrant and cheerful as ever.

That's the nature of spring snow. It's depressing—but it never stays very long. And why not? Because it's falling on a warm world, and all that warmth just melts it away.

It sort of seems to mirror my life, really. For example, I have had a horrendous week. Things have been crazy at work: a whole blizzard of deadlines and last-minute changes to projects and demands on my time and emotional energy.

Top it off with the fact that we're remodeling our house, so going home is not exactly a respite. It generally involves fighting through a layer of dust to clear a spot on the range, washing pans in the bathtub before and after using them, searching through boxes to find the cutting board and the garlic salt and a fork to stir the potatoes with.

Sometimes, when I have a week like this, it seems like I'll never be calm again. Other times, the frustration falls and falls, but it just seems to melt away. What makes the difference? The warmth in my heart.

The person I really want to be is one who has springtime in her heart all the time. Then, when the blizzard comes, it may be unpleasant for a moment, but it will quickly fade away, leaving only the moisture that makes my life even more fruitful than it would have been otherwise. But even when it's winter, and the snow sticks around for a long, long time, I take heart in knowing that spring *will* come. The Son shines in my soul today, glorious and bright. May it ever be so for you!

.